GEOMETRIC
DESIGNS
COLORING BOOK

HOP DAVID

PETER VON THENEN

DOVER PUBLICATIONS, INC.
MINEOLA, NEW YORK

Bibliographical Note

Geometric Designs Coloring Book is a new compilation of designs from the following previously published Dover books: *Geoscapes* (Designs 1–31) by Hop David and *Prismatic Designs* (Designs 32–62) by Peter Von Thenen.

International Standard Book Number

ISBN-13: 978-0-486-80350-0
ISBN-10: 0-486-80350-3

Manufactured in the United States by RR Donnelley
80350304   2015
www.doverpublications.com

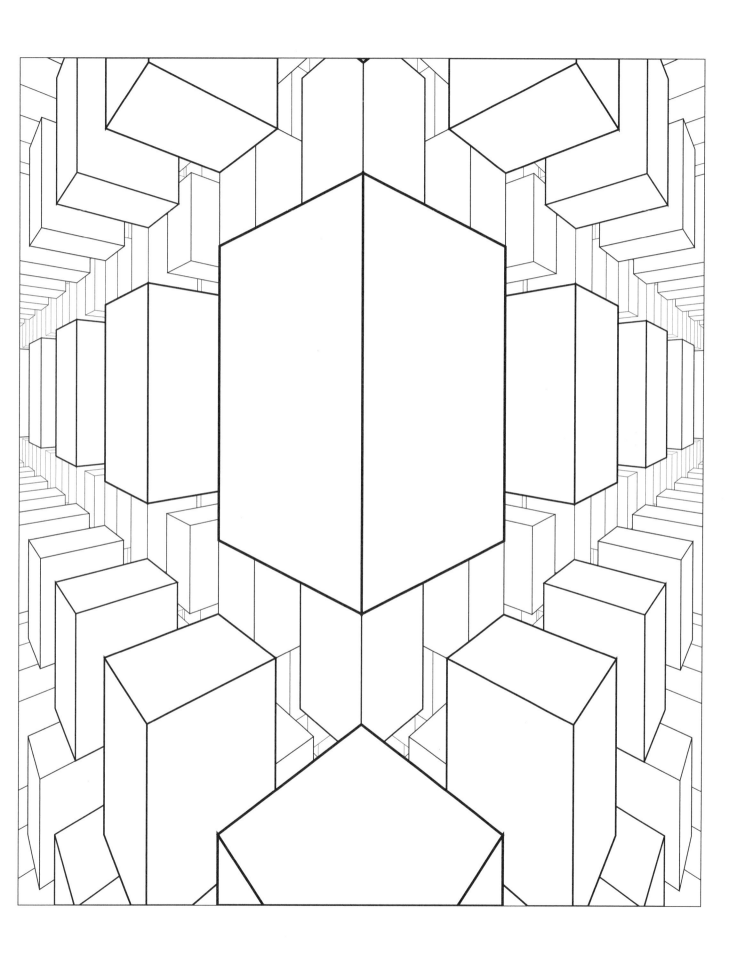

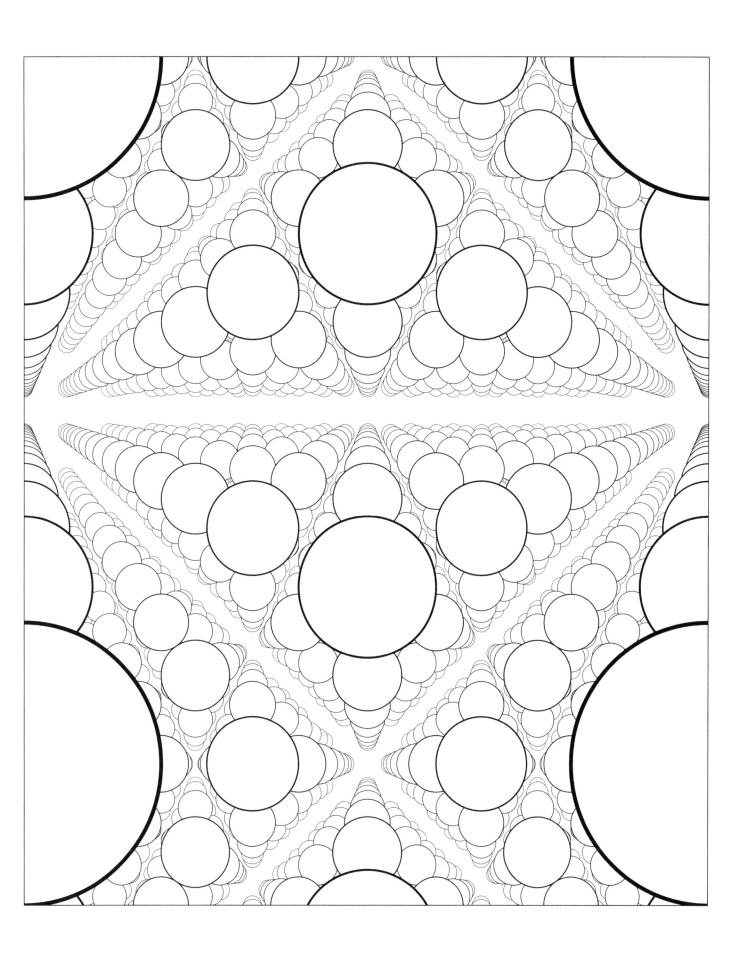

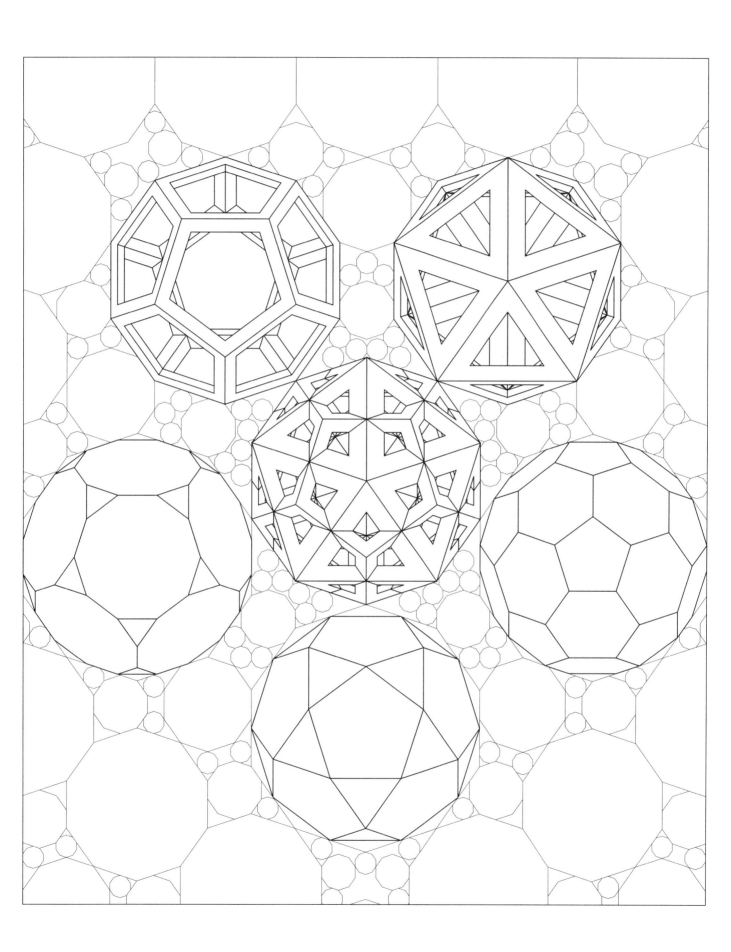

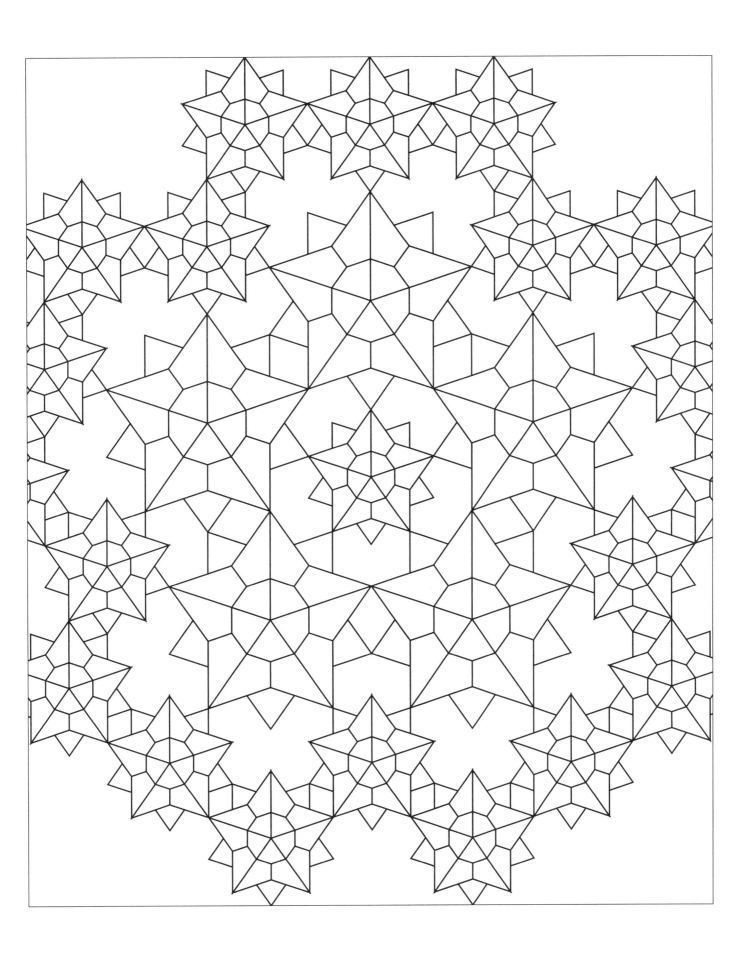

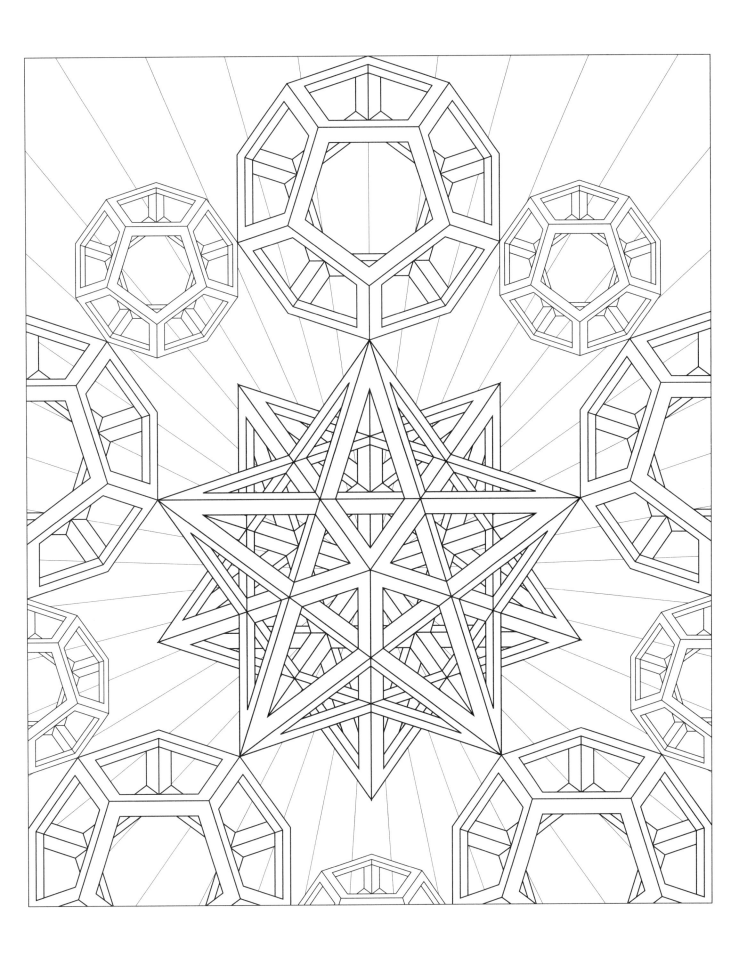

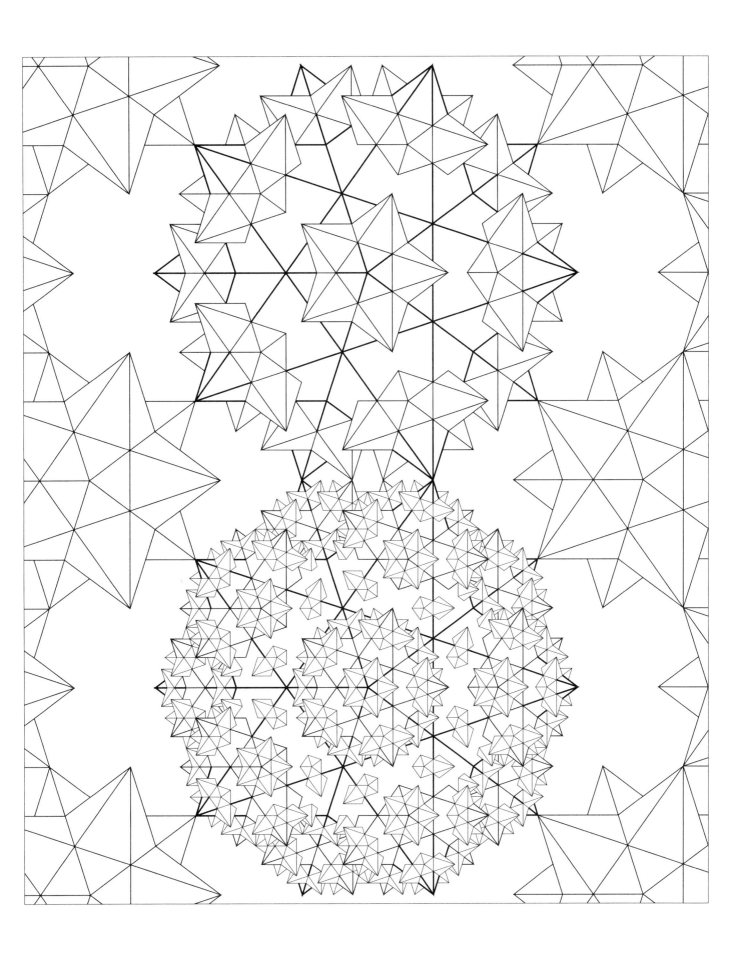

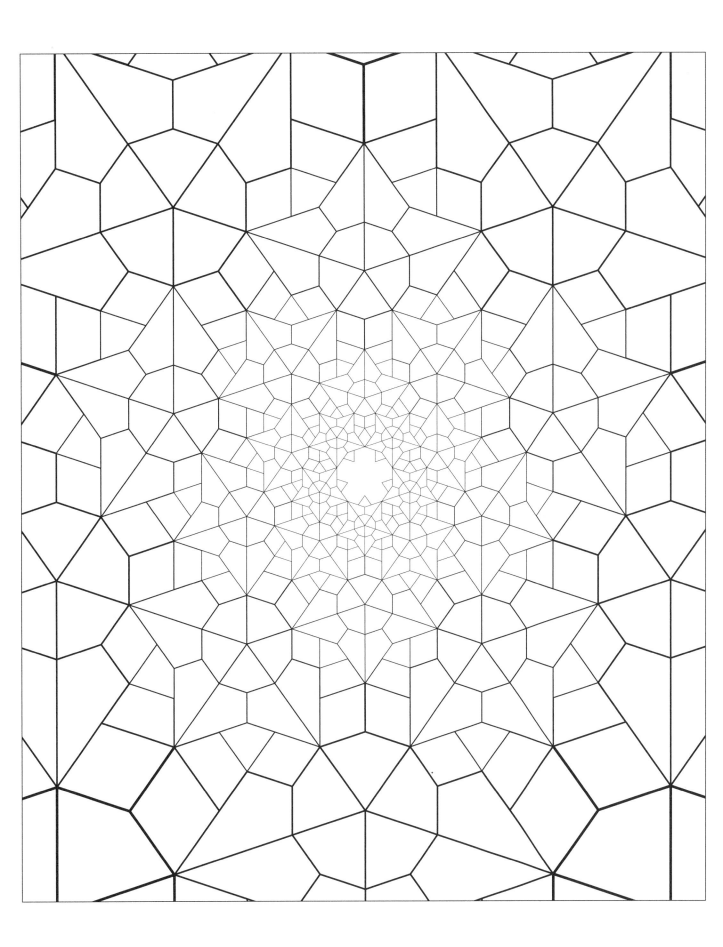

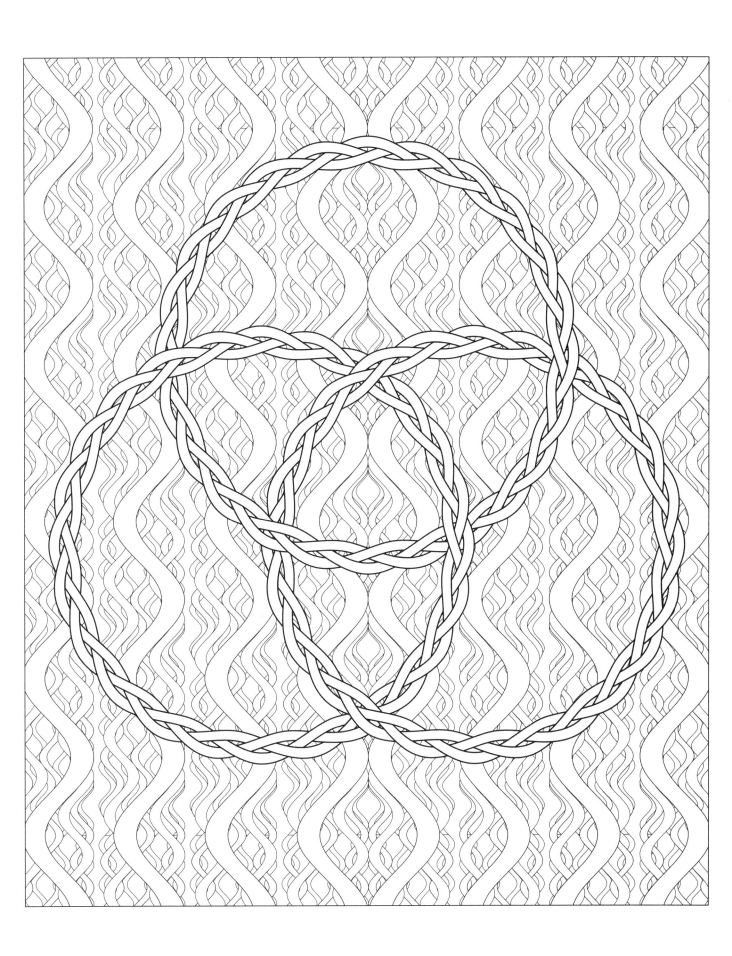

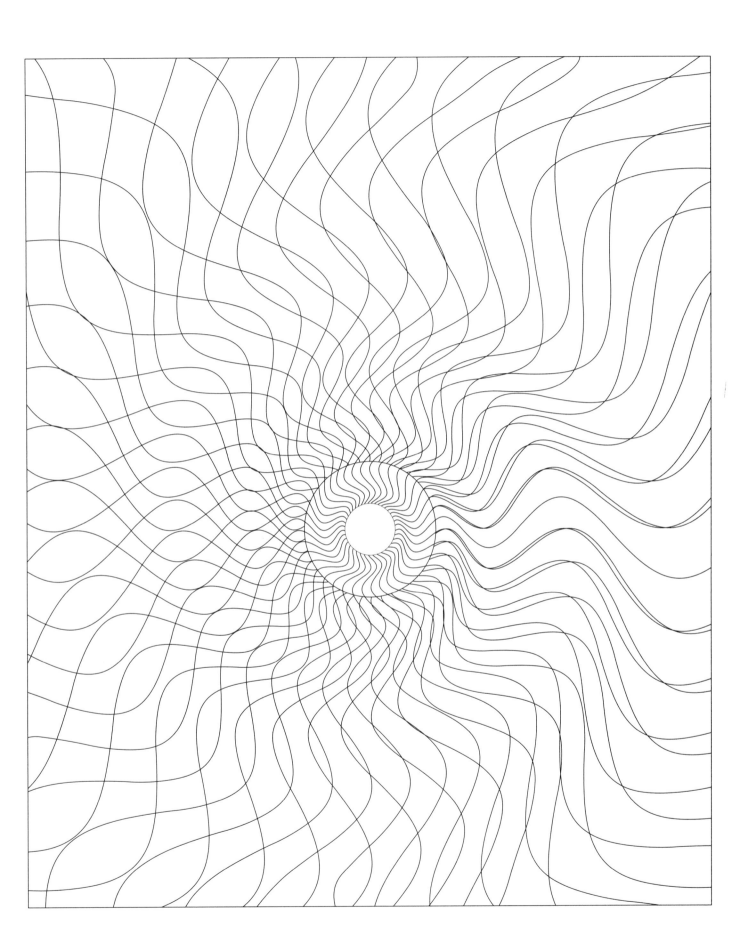

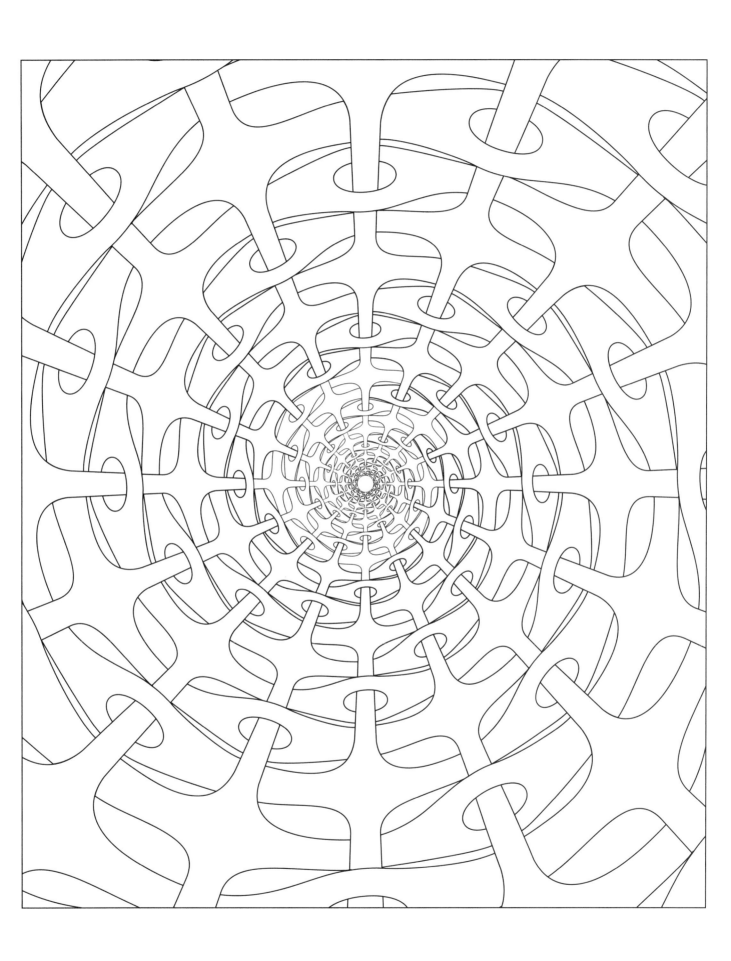

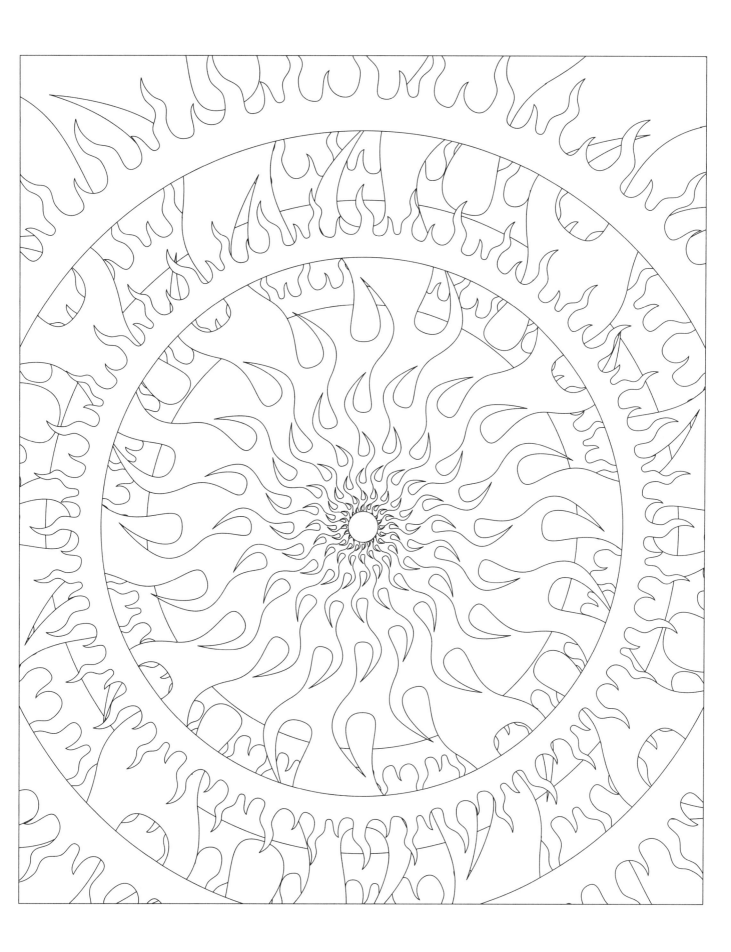

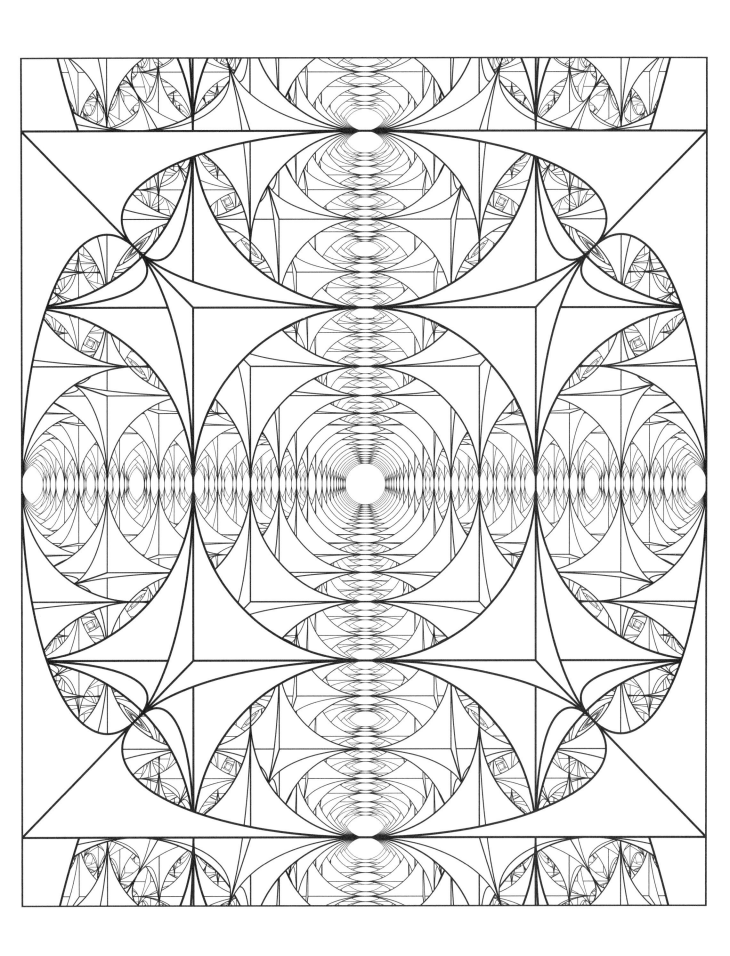

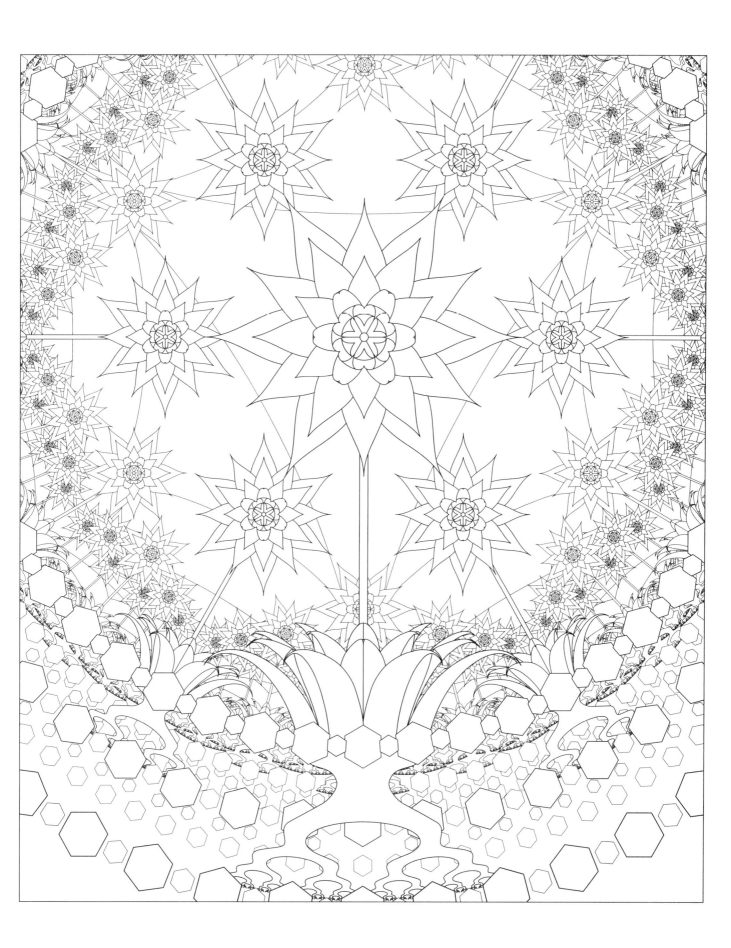

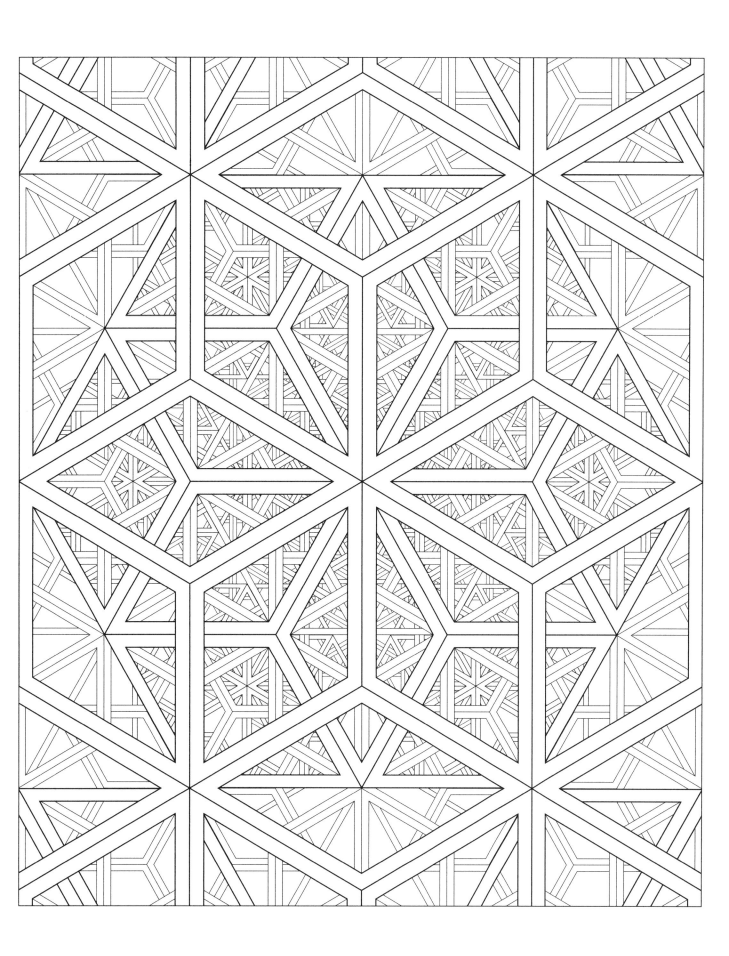

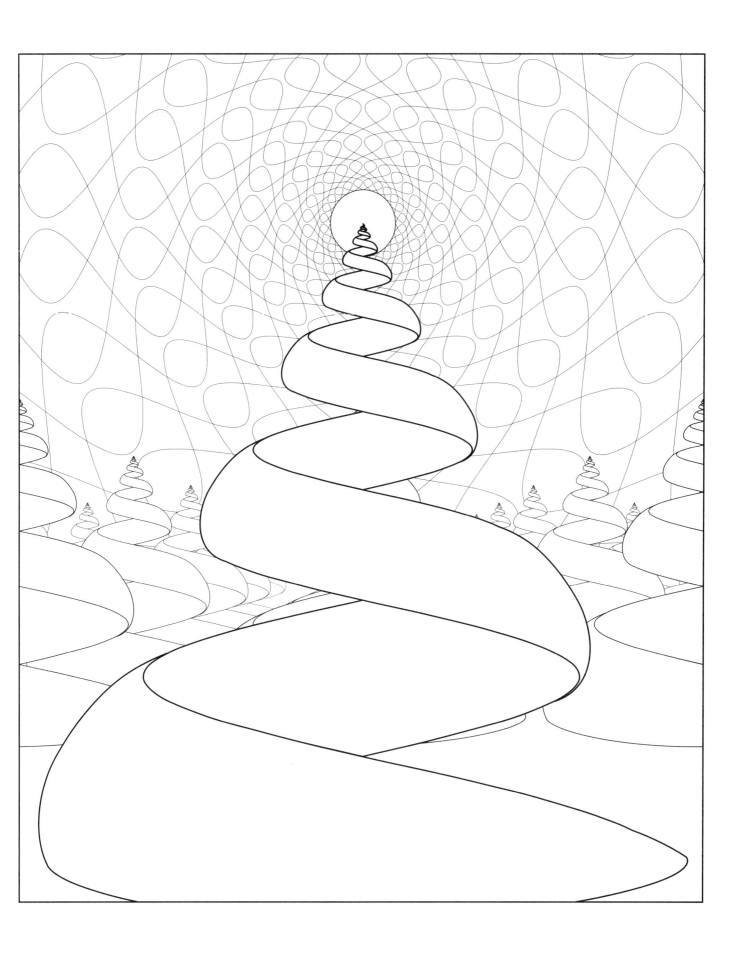

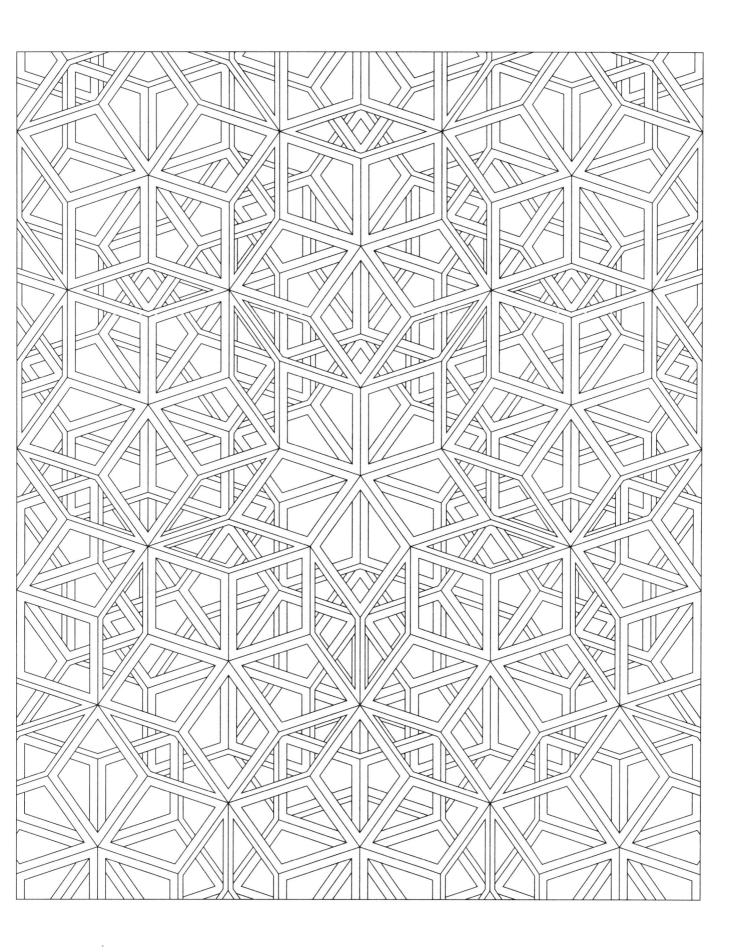

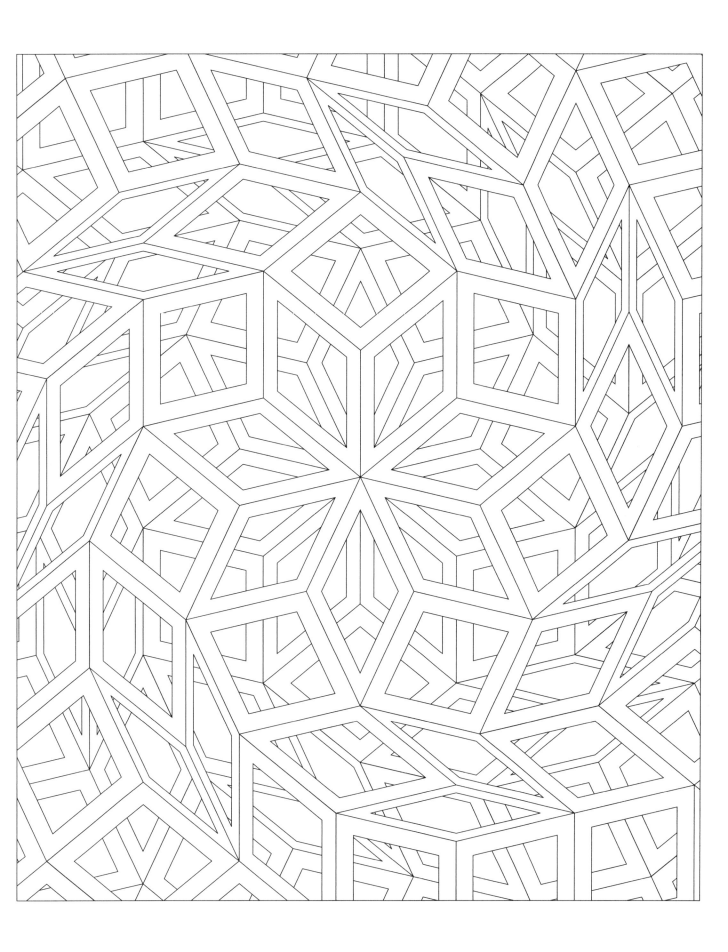

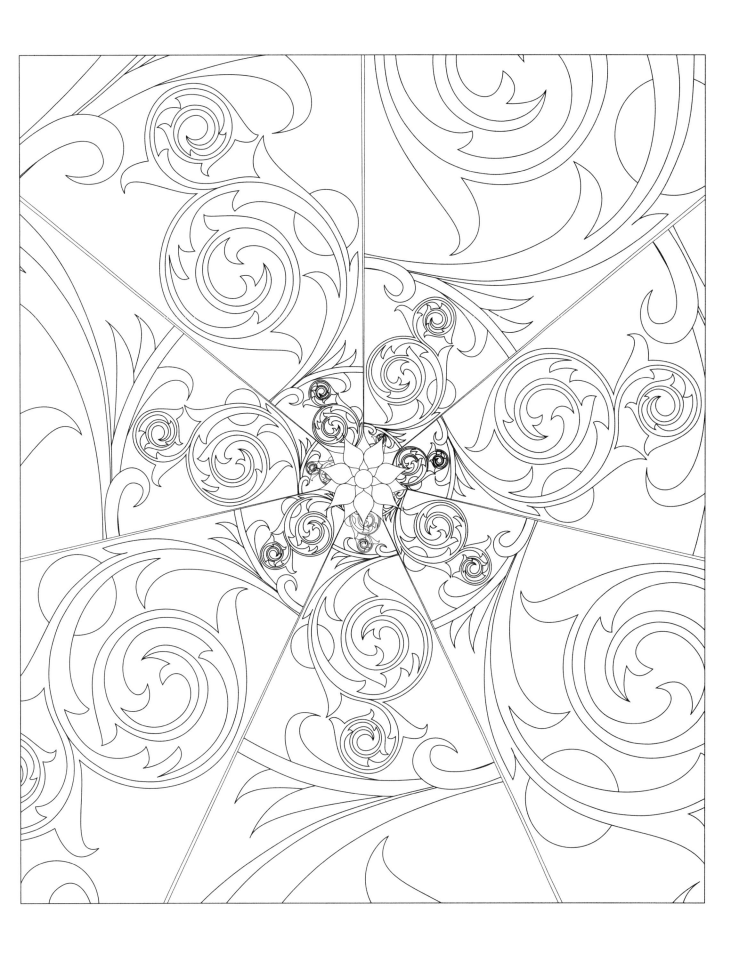

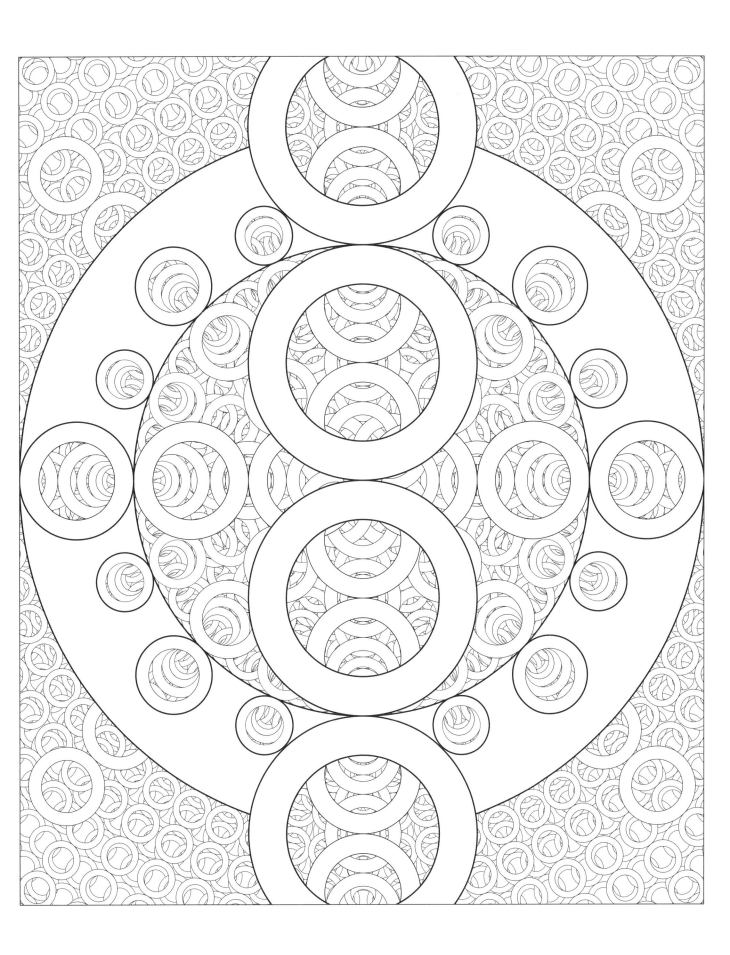

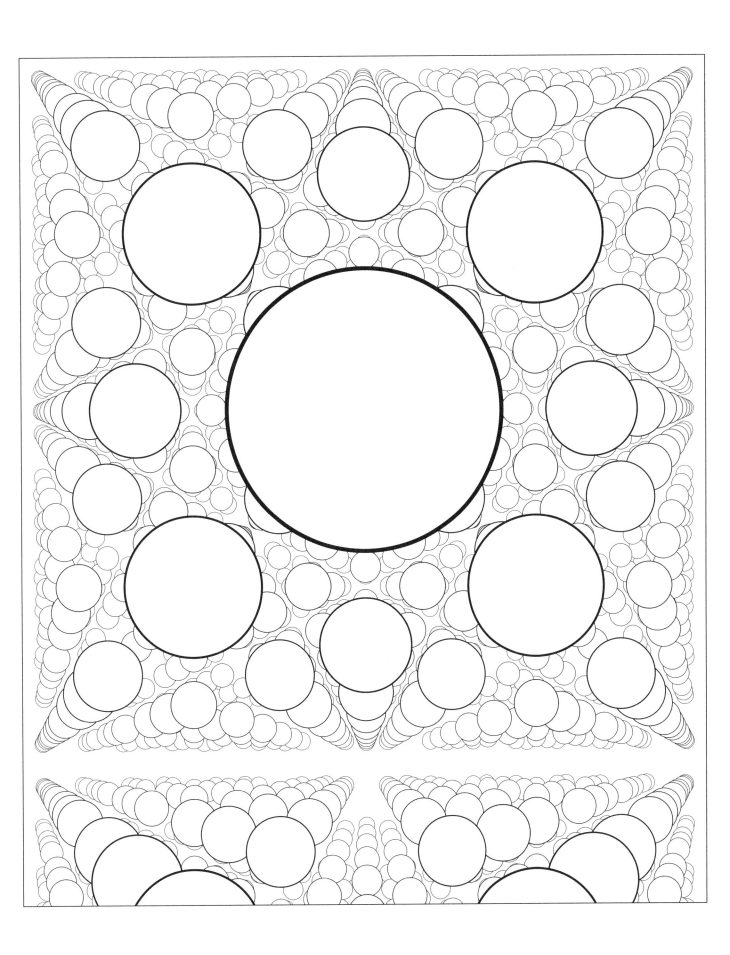

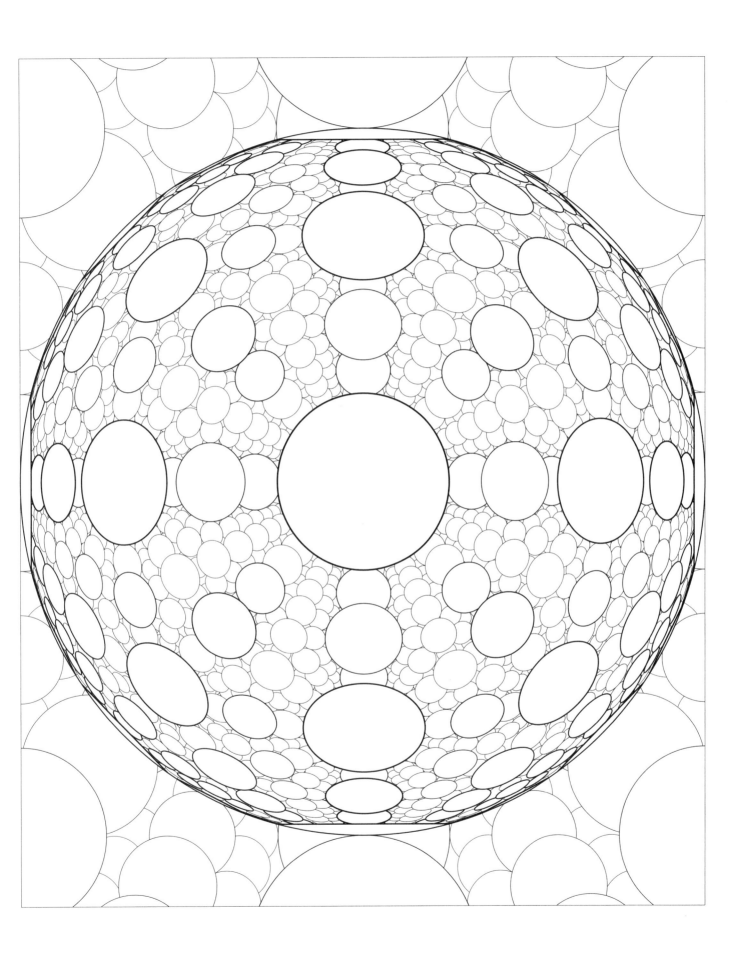

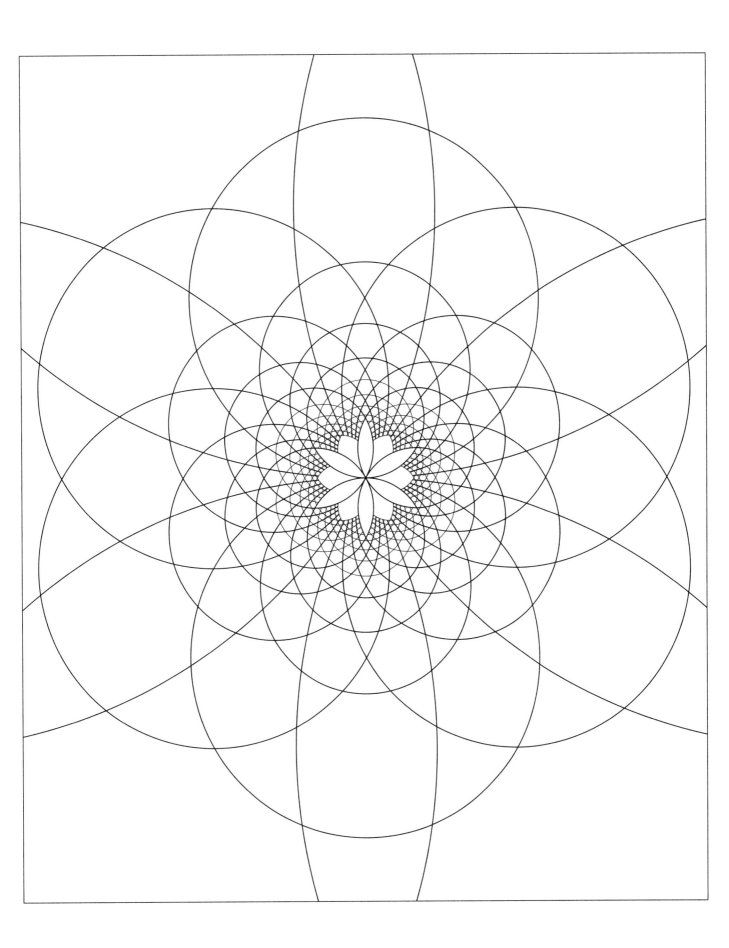

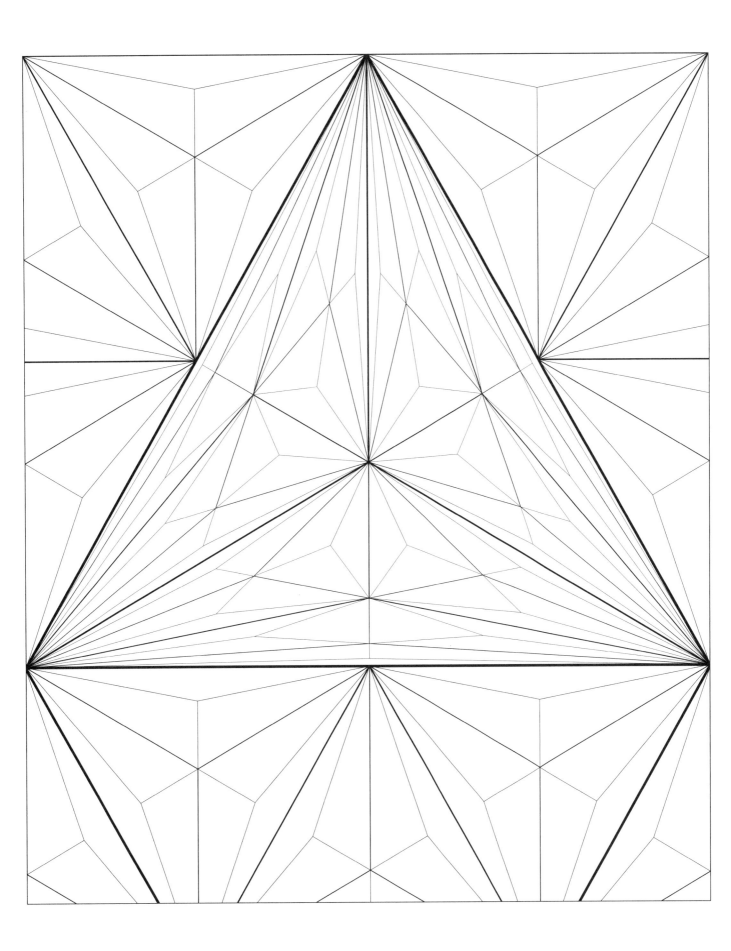

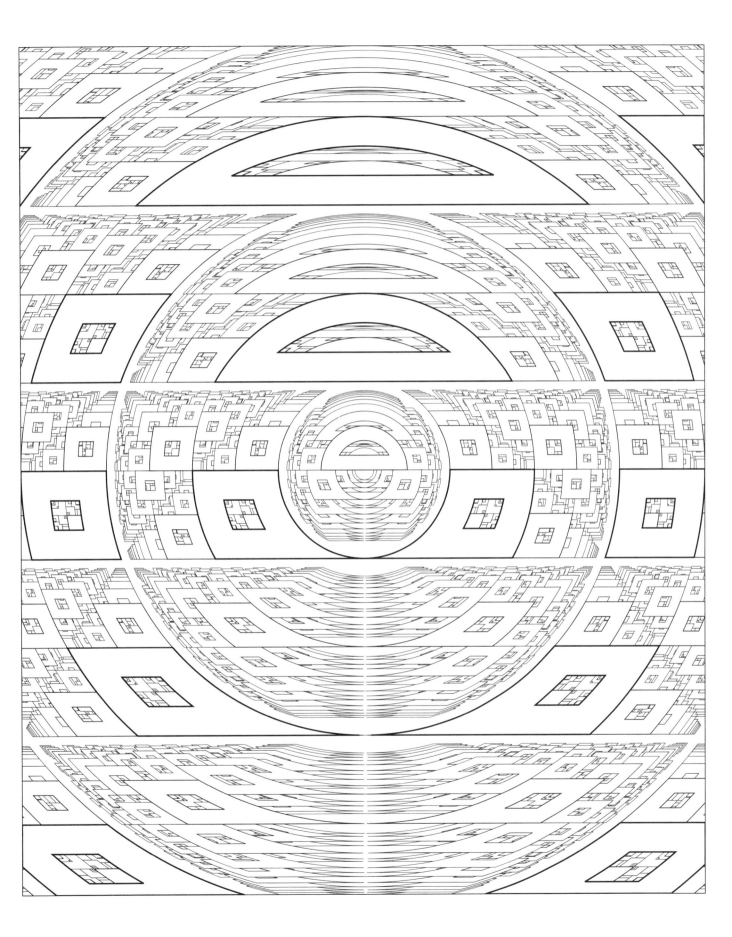

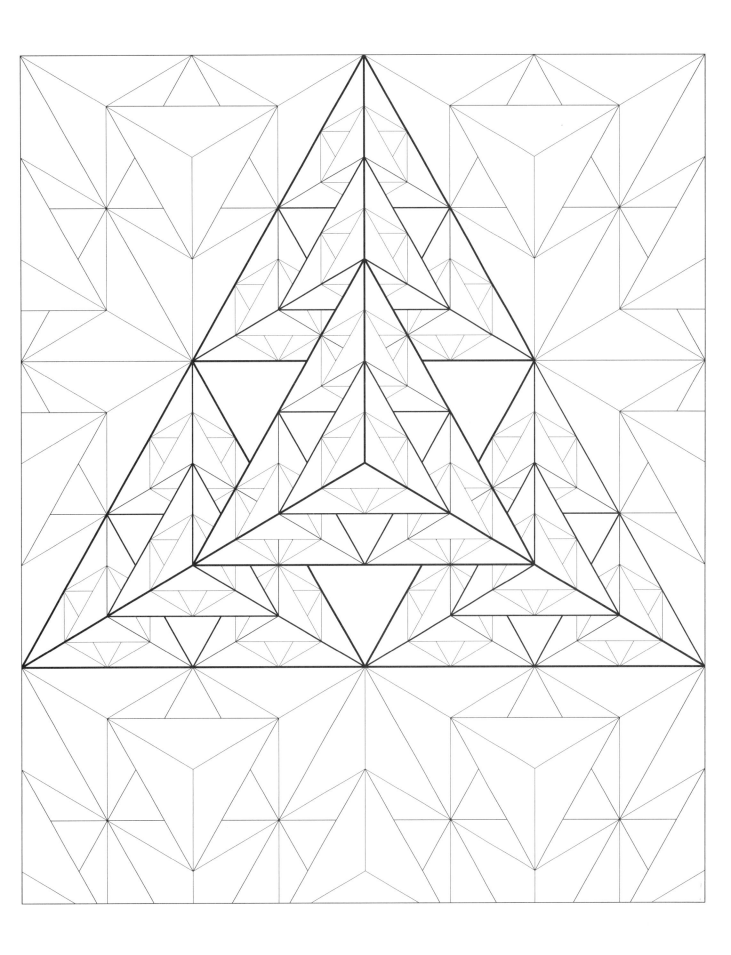

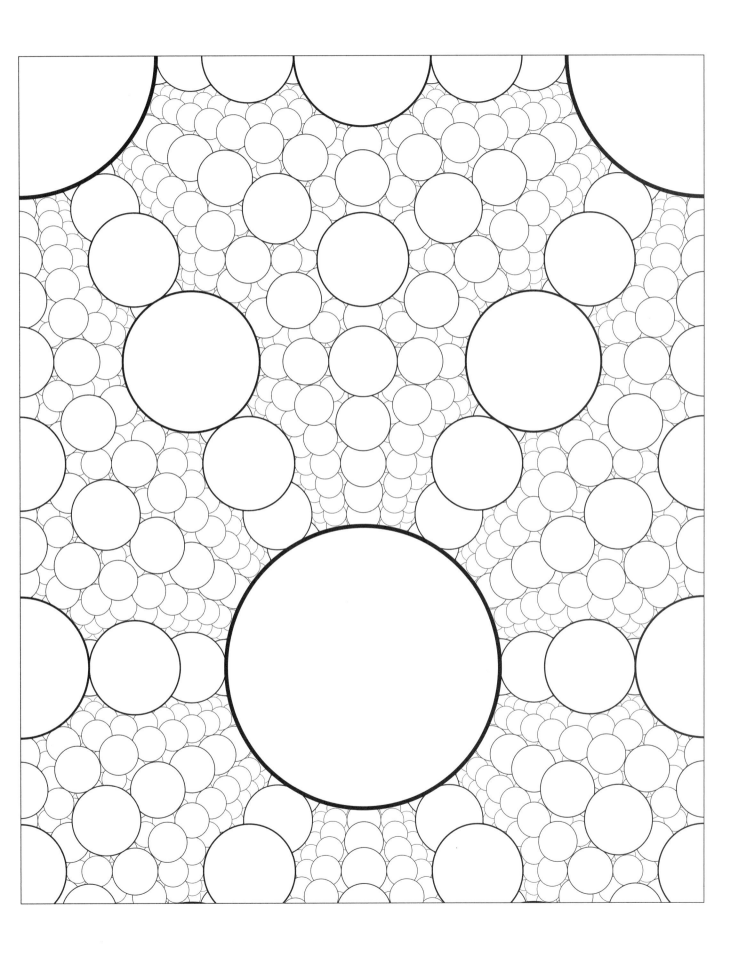

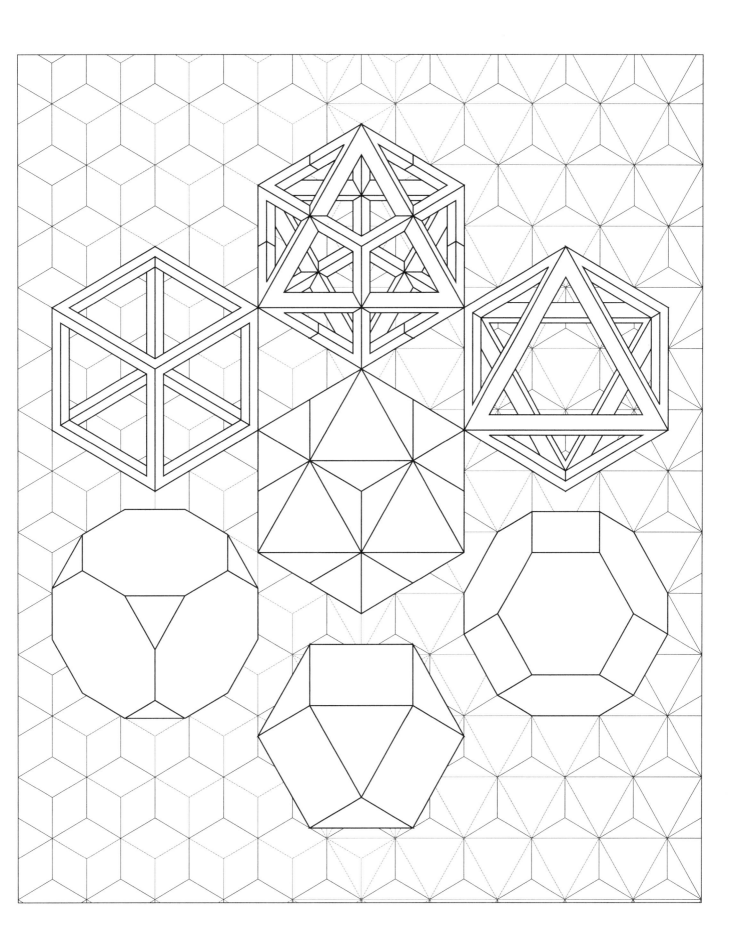

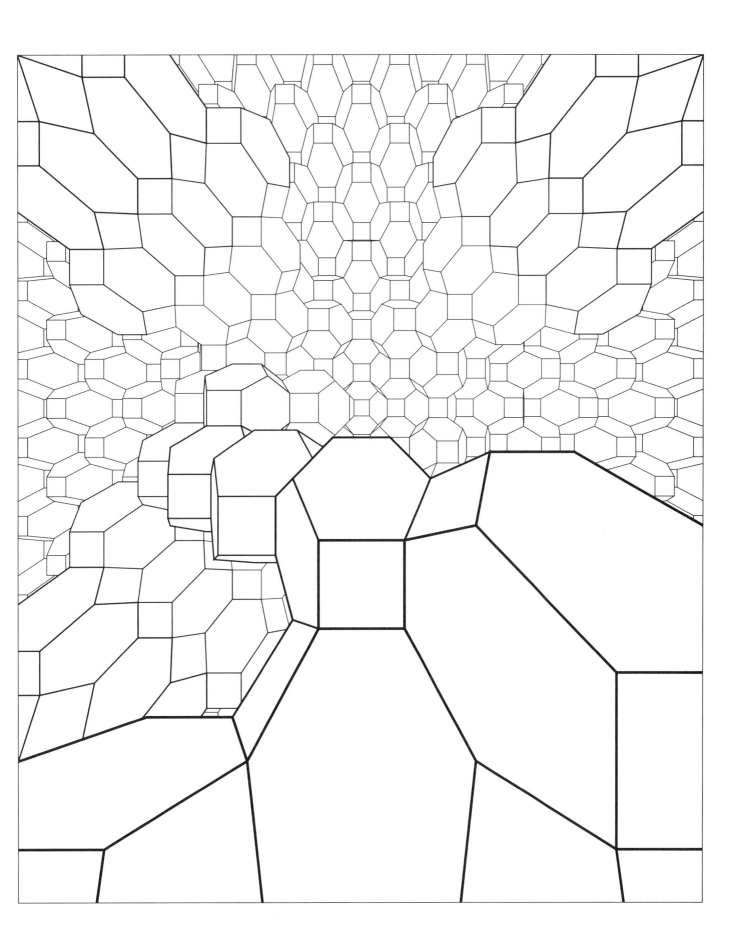

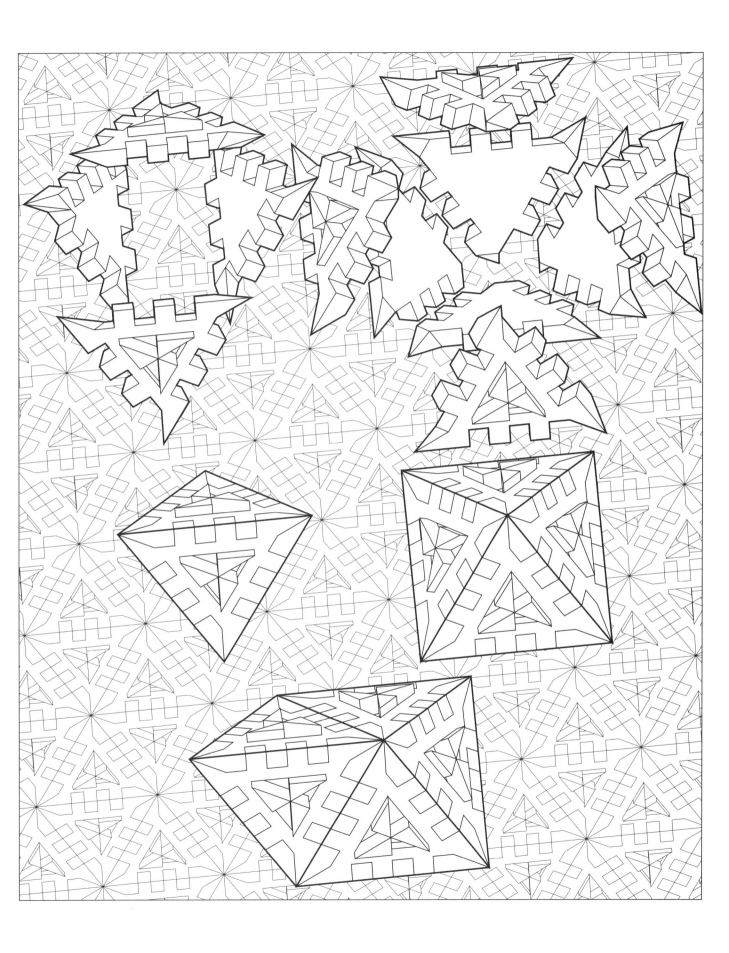

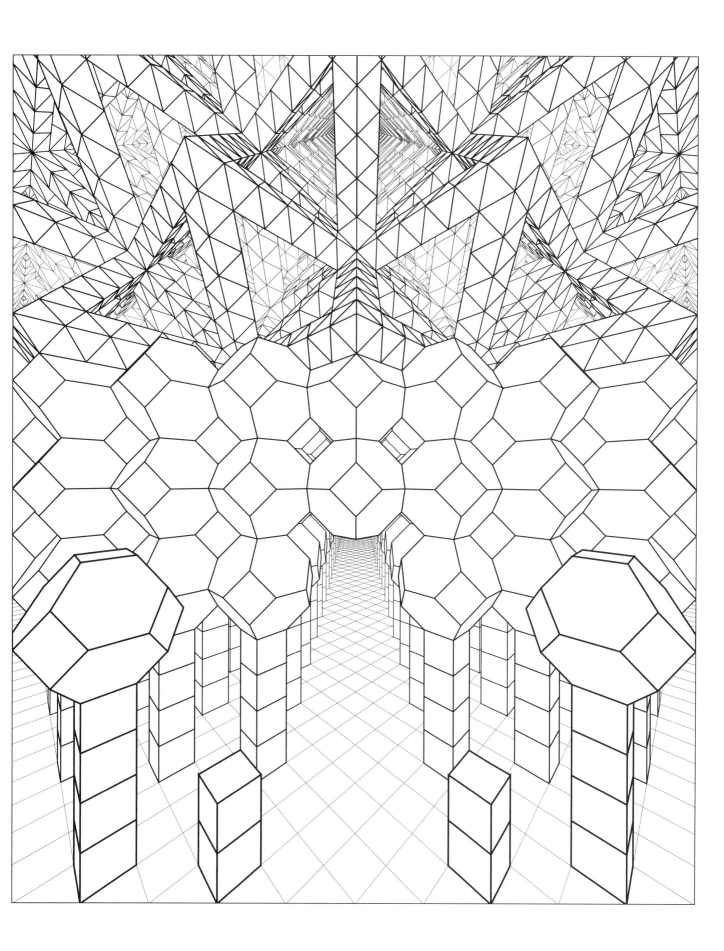

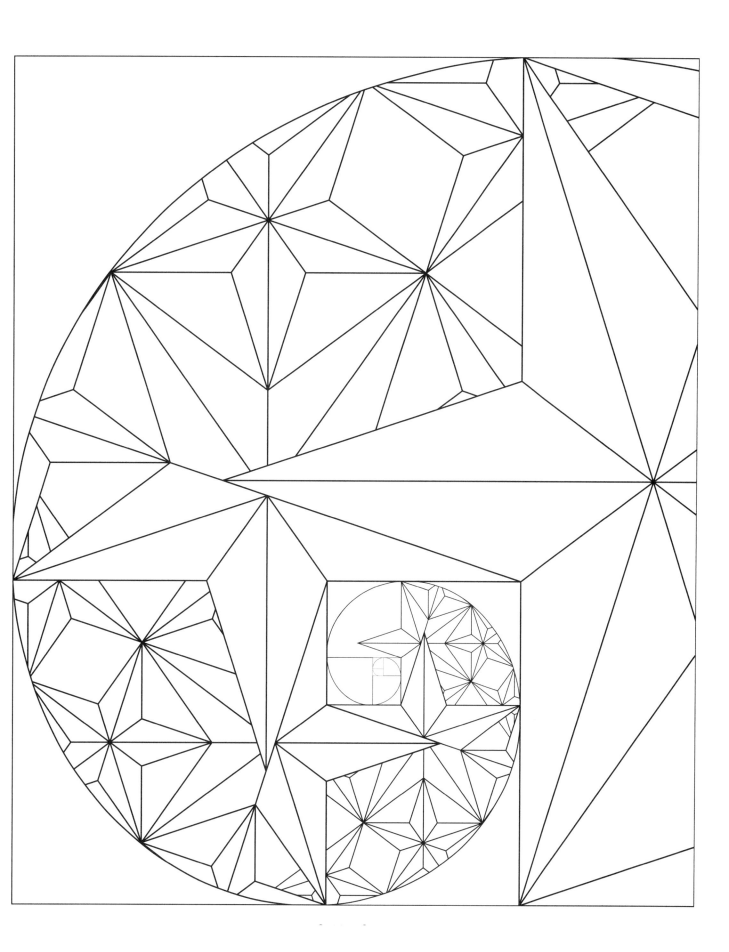

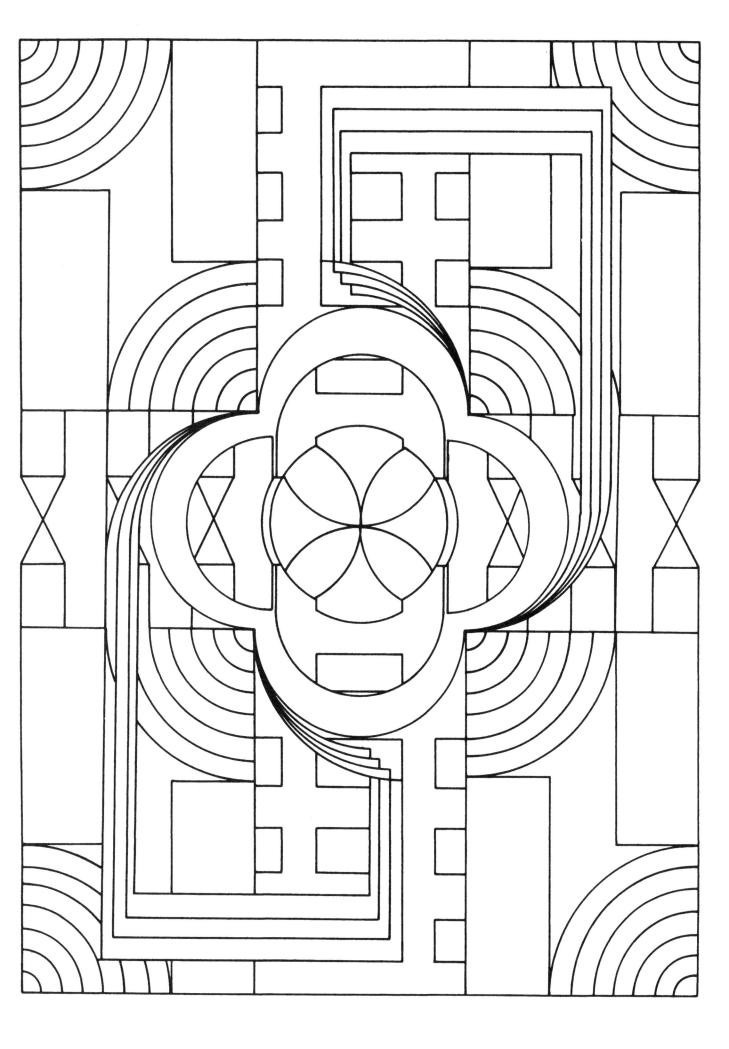

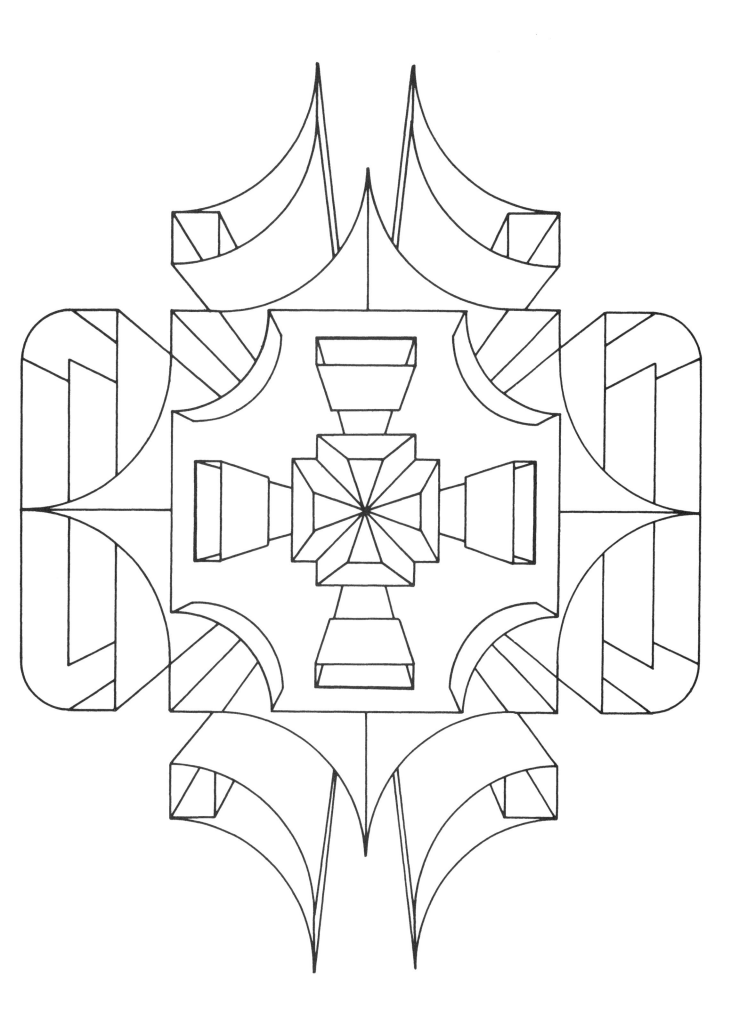

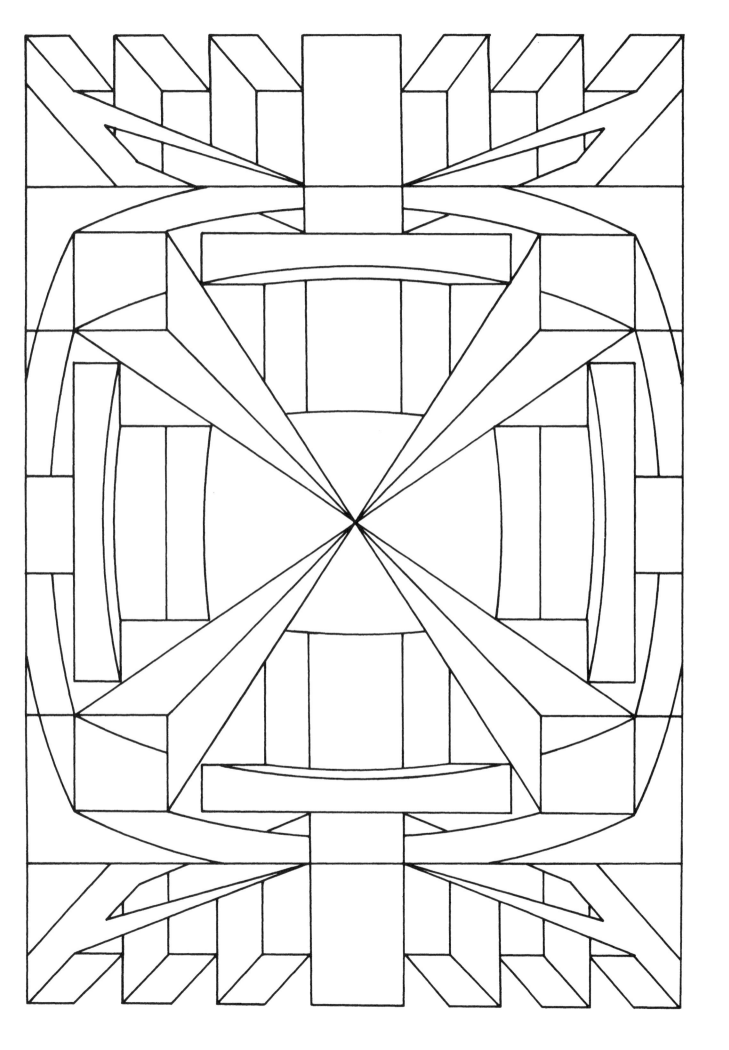

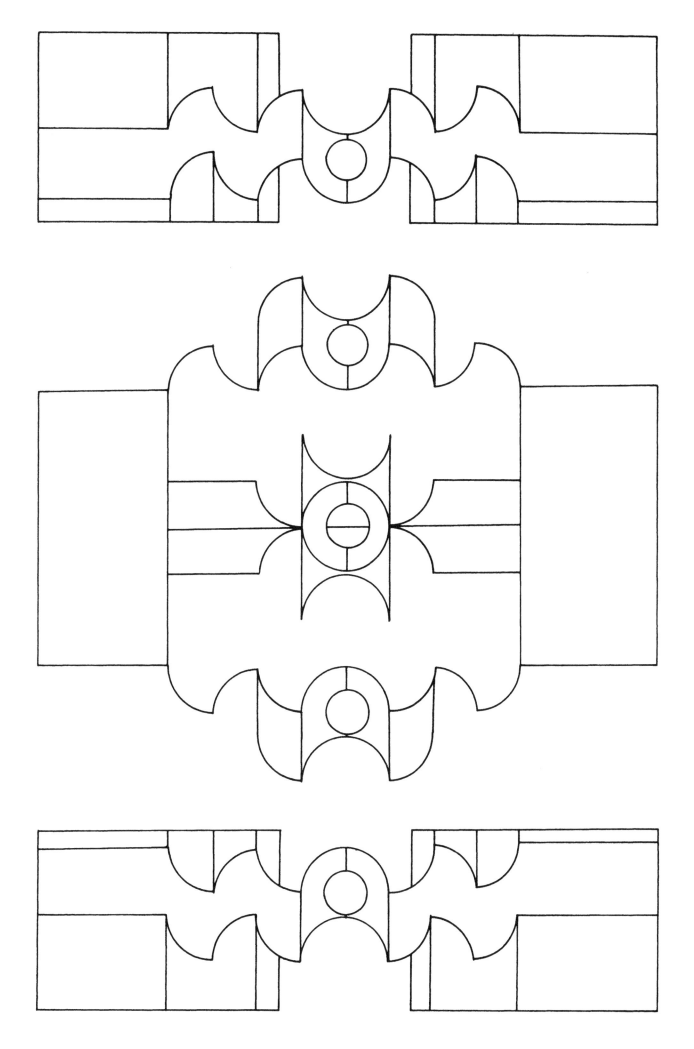

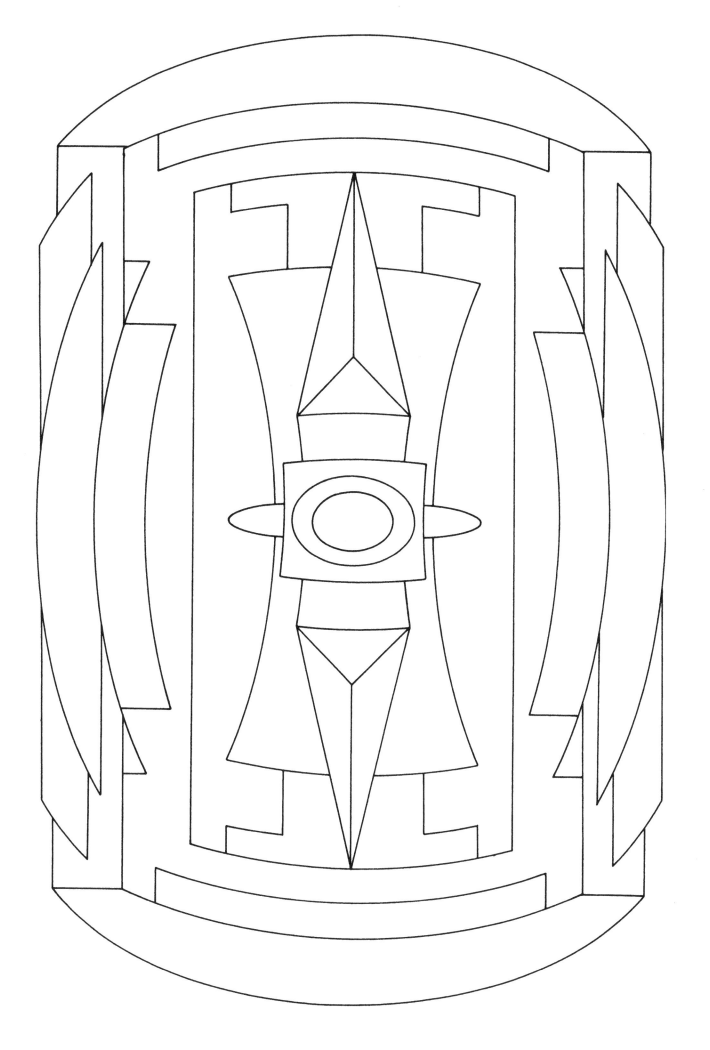

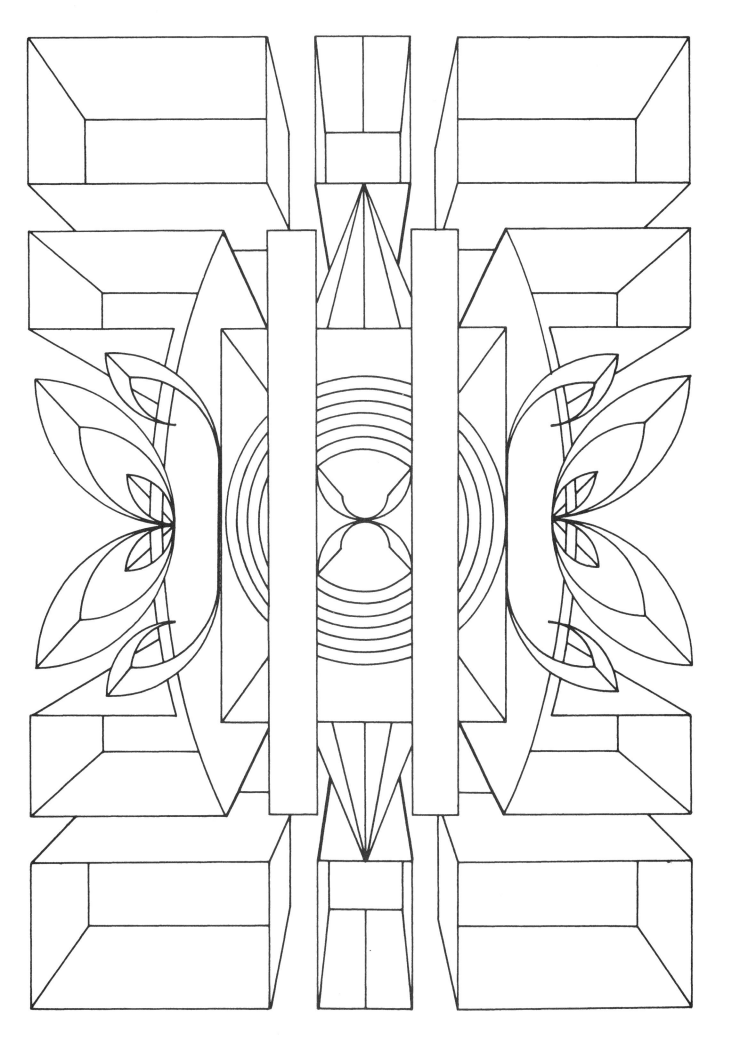

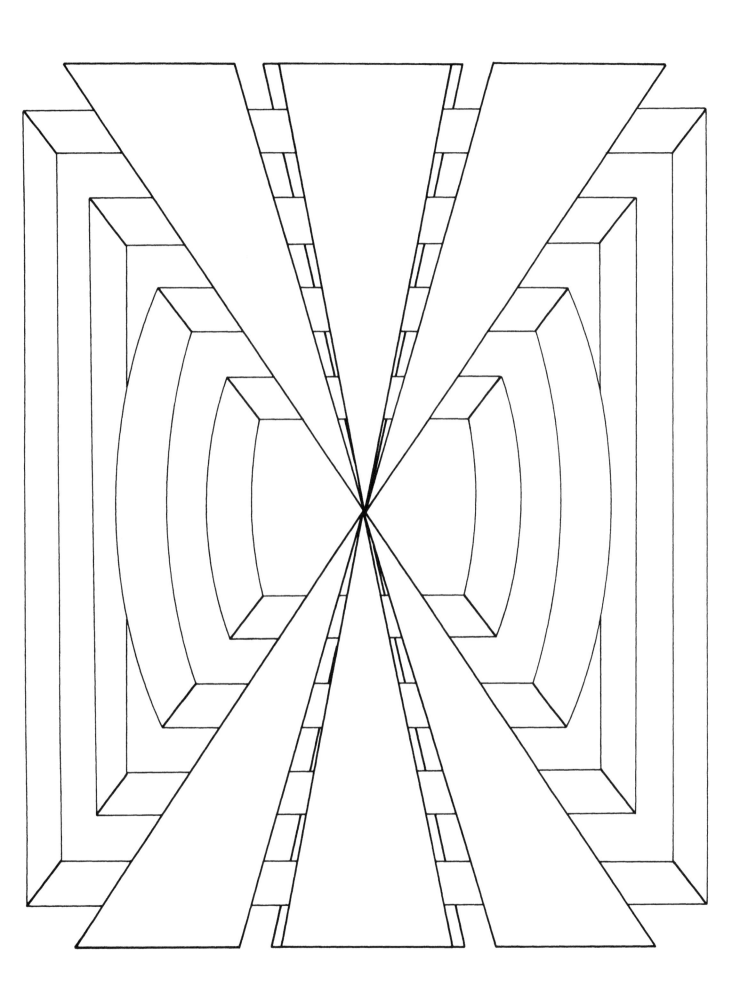

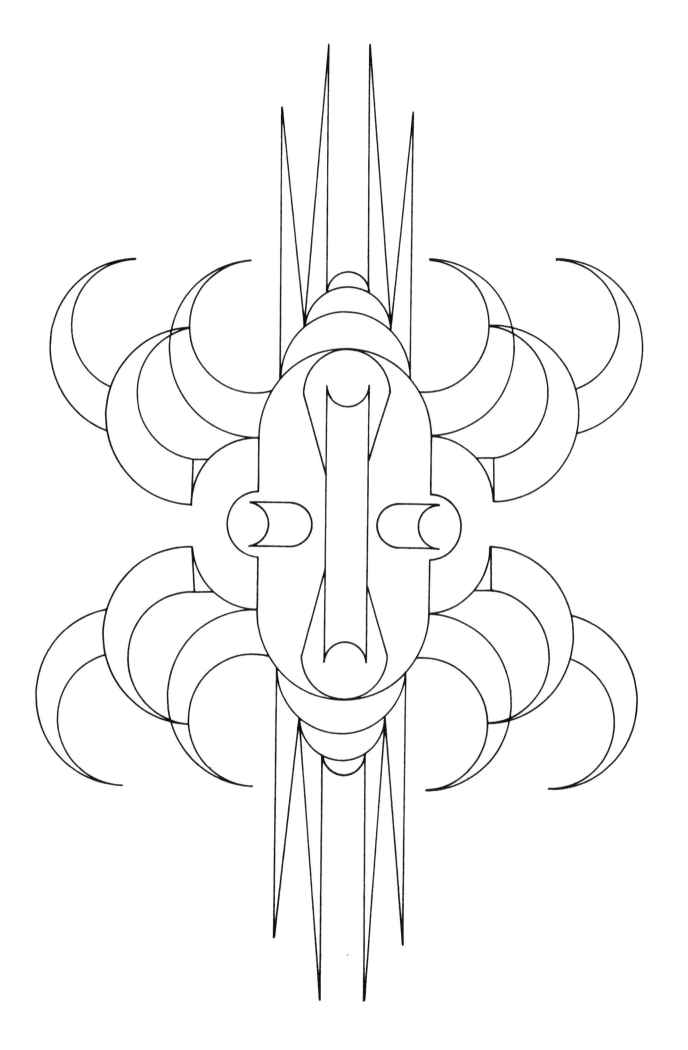

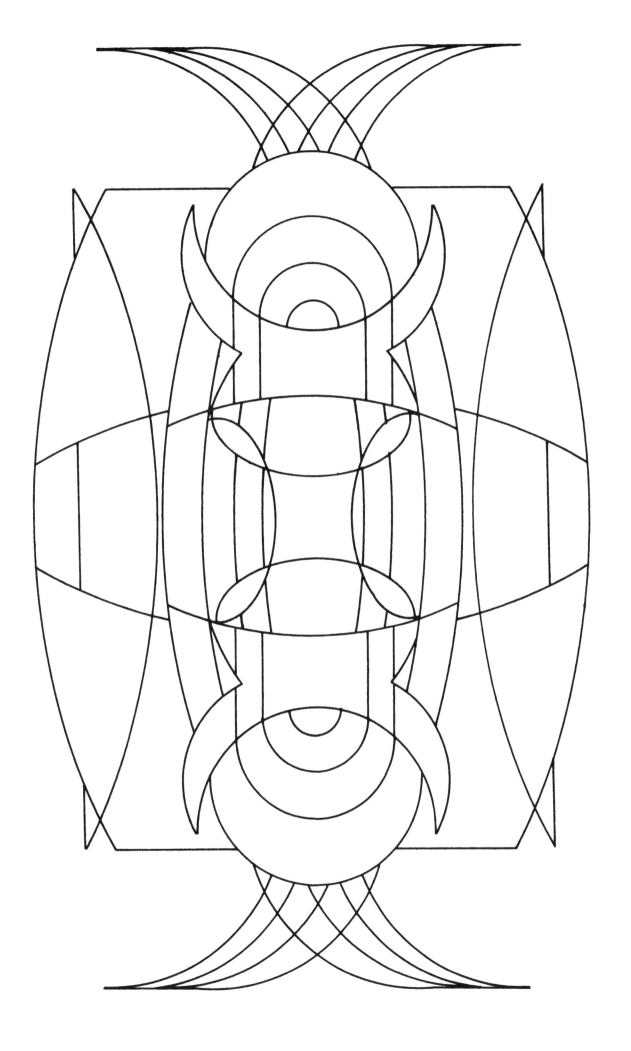

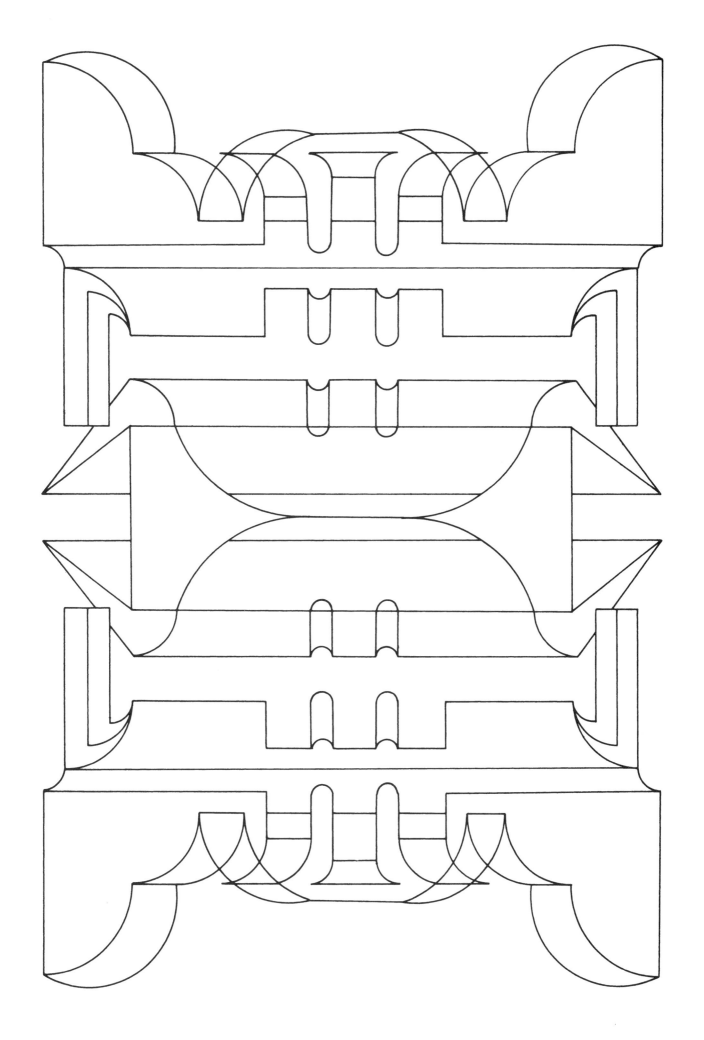

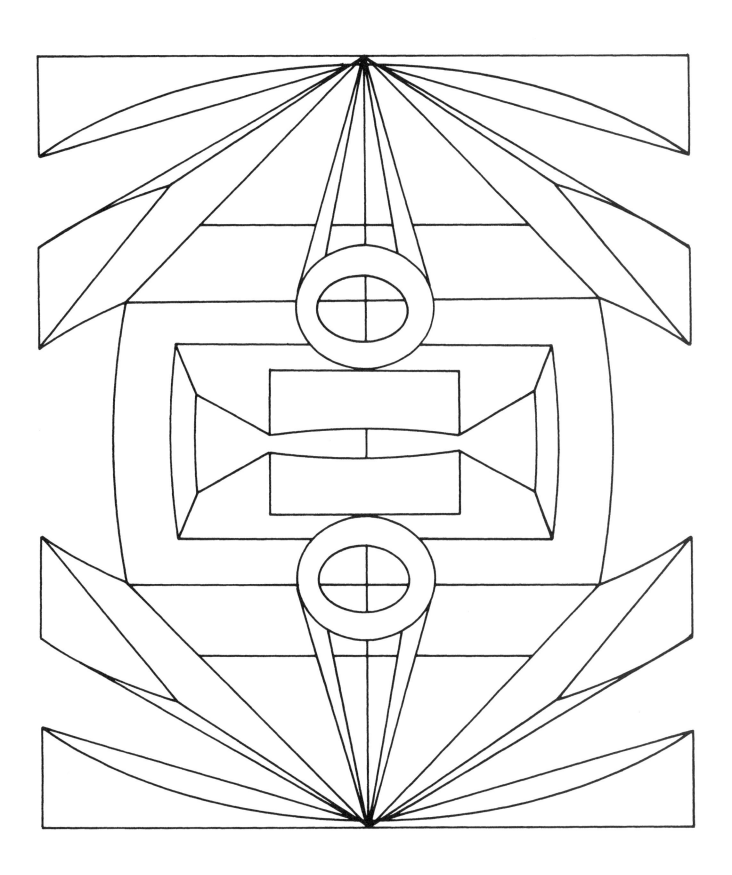

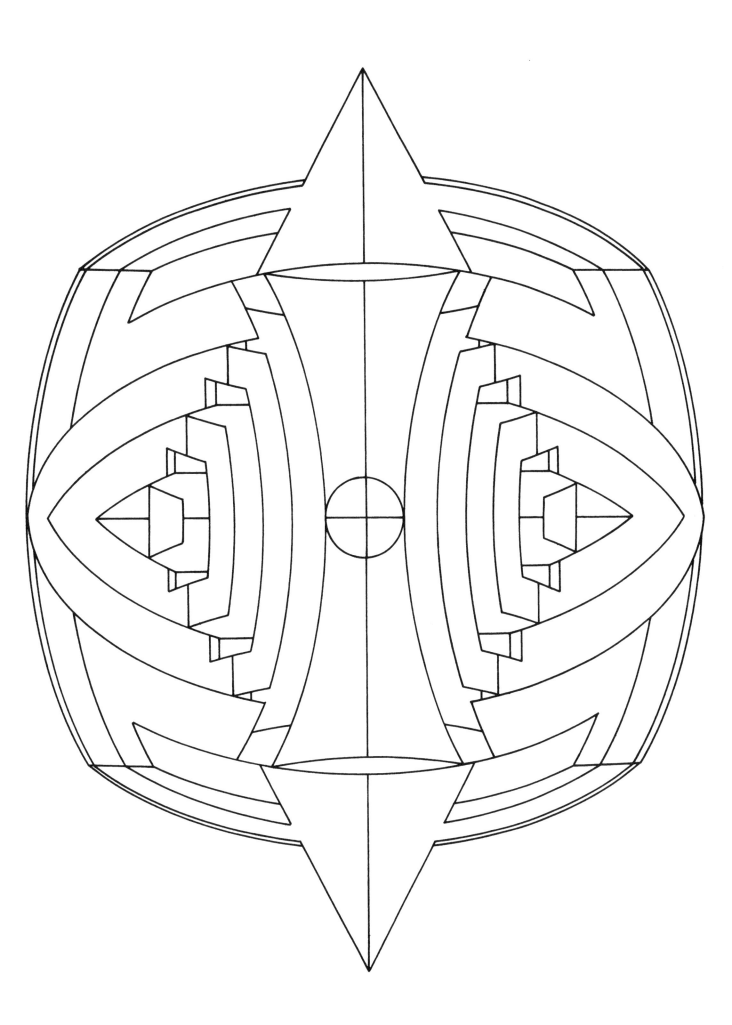

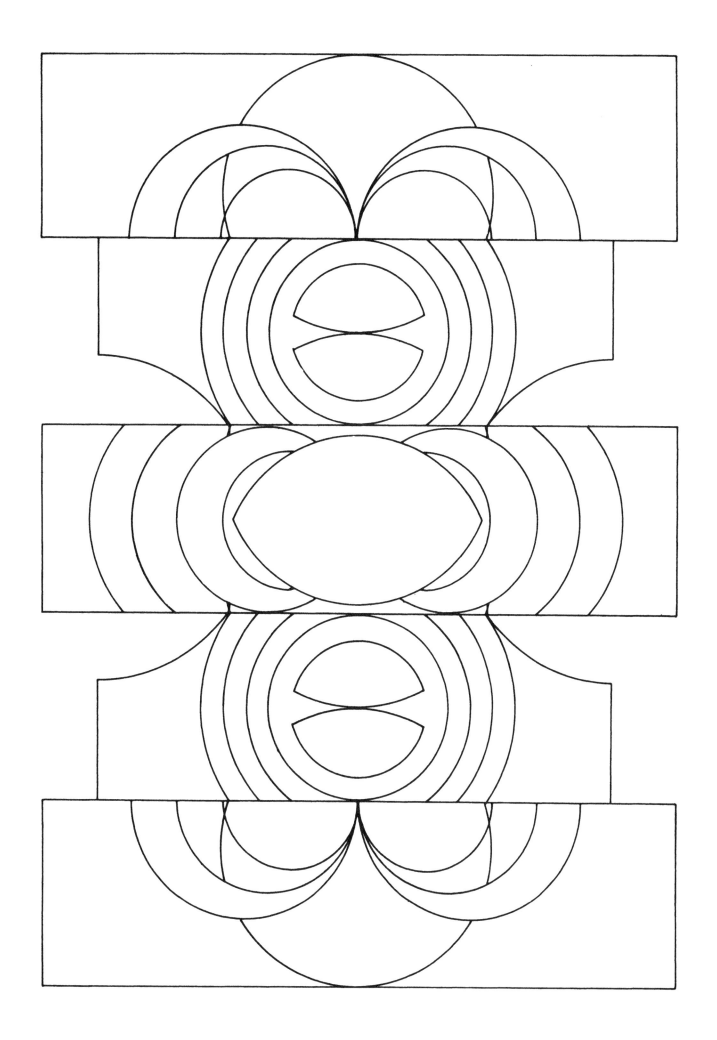

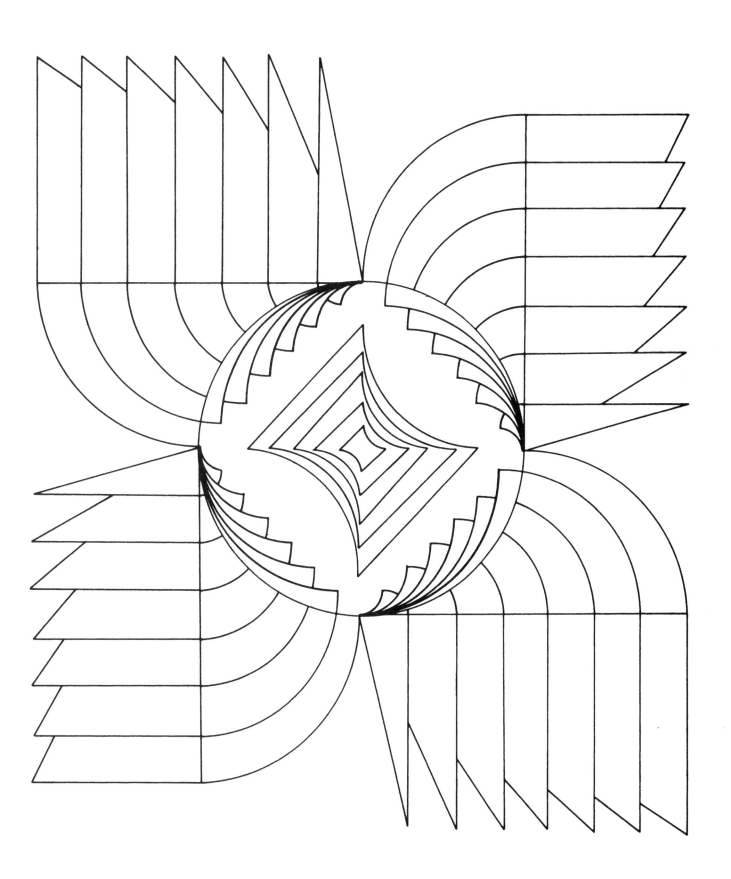

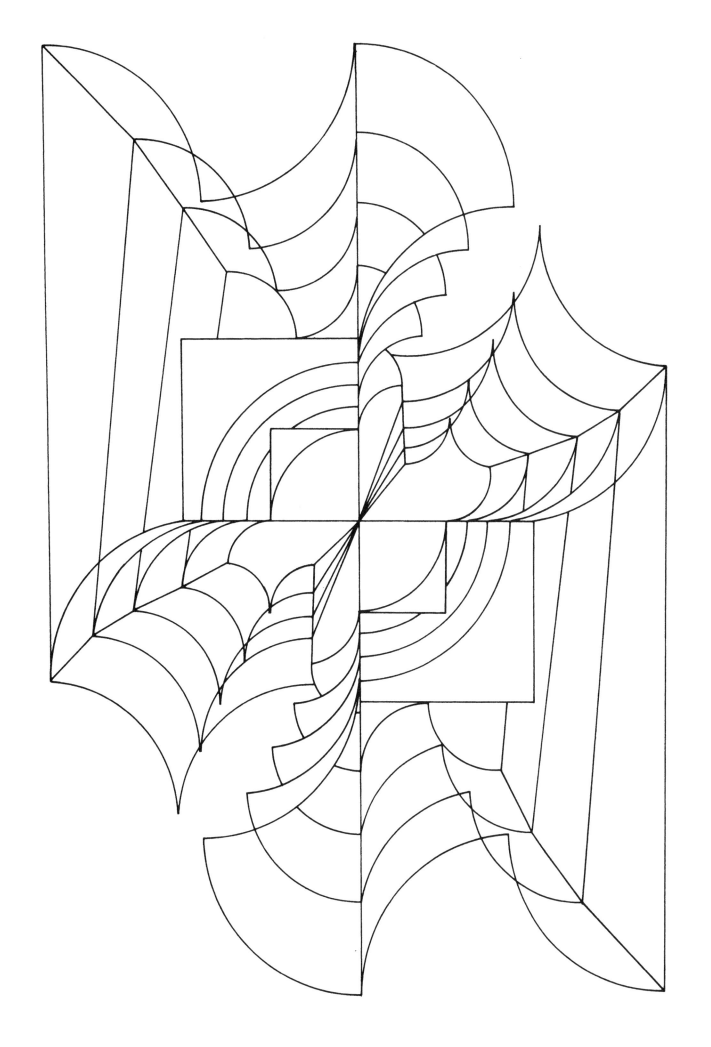

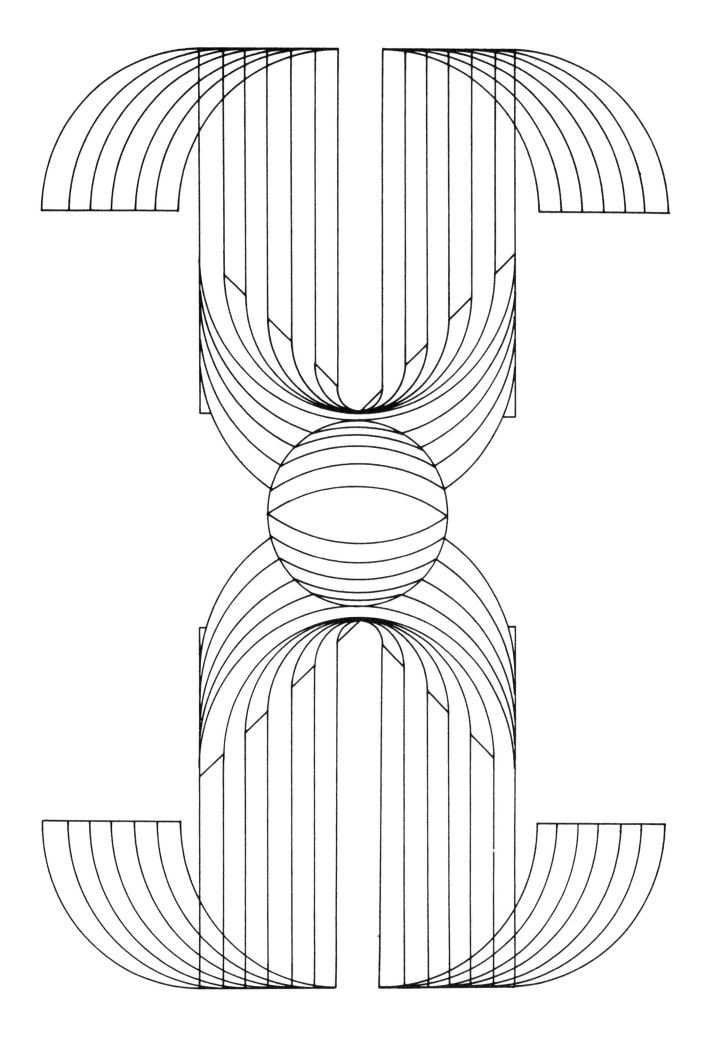

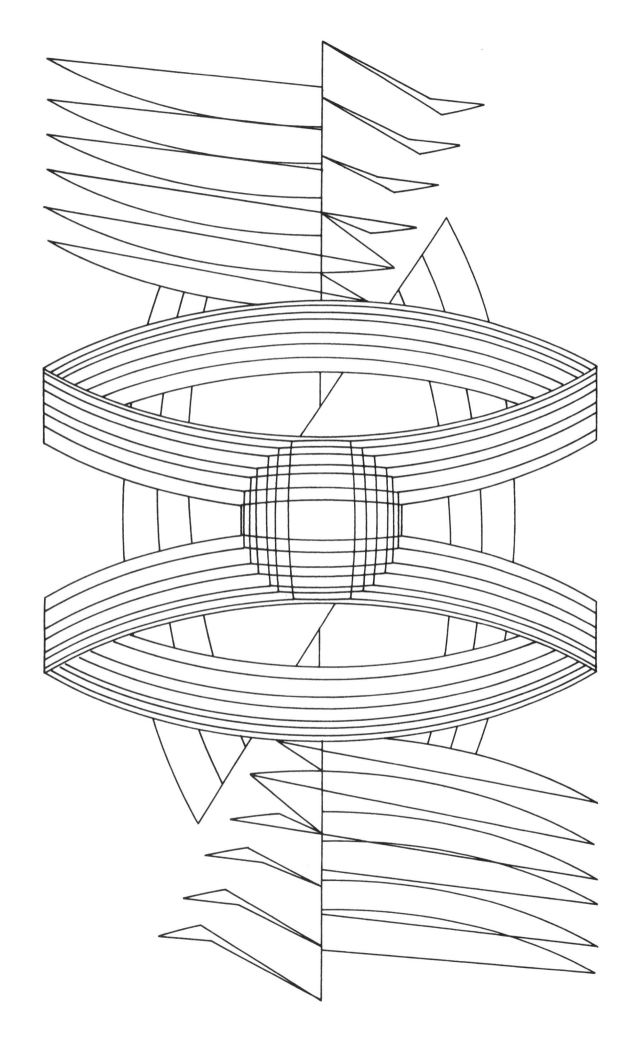

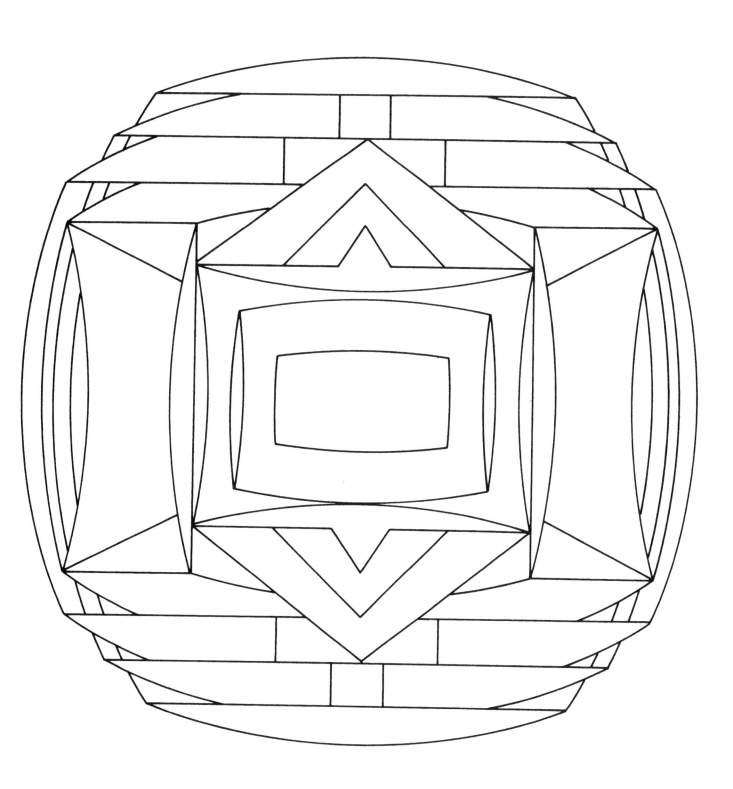

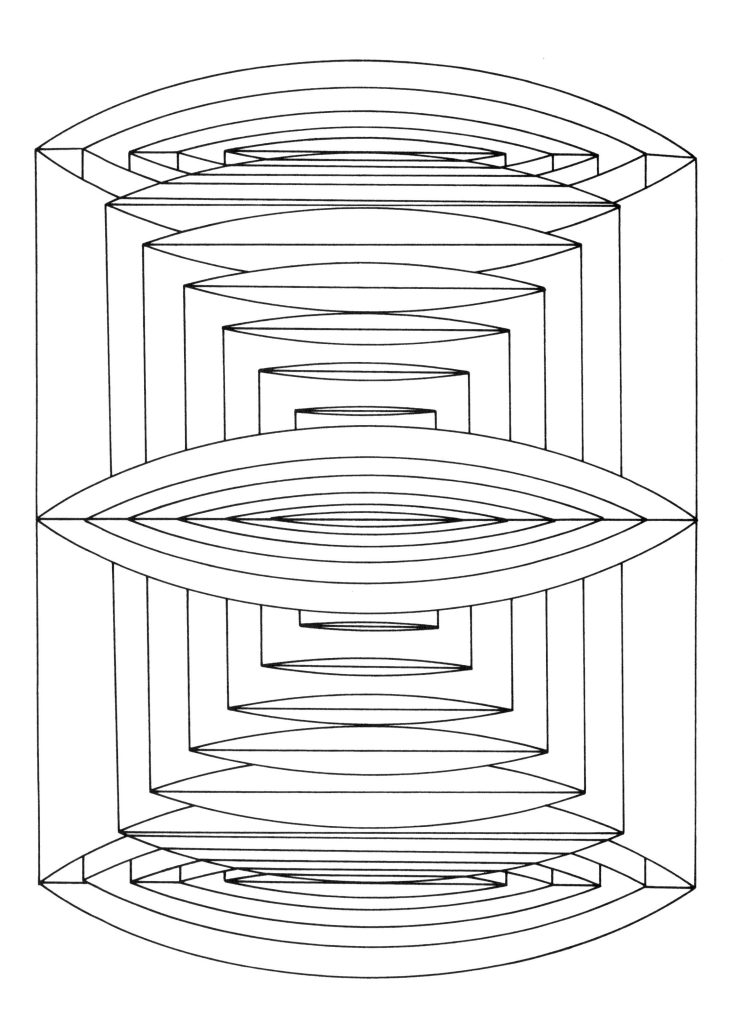

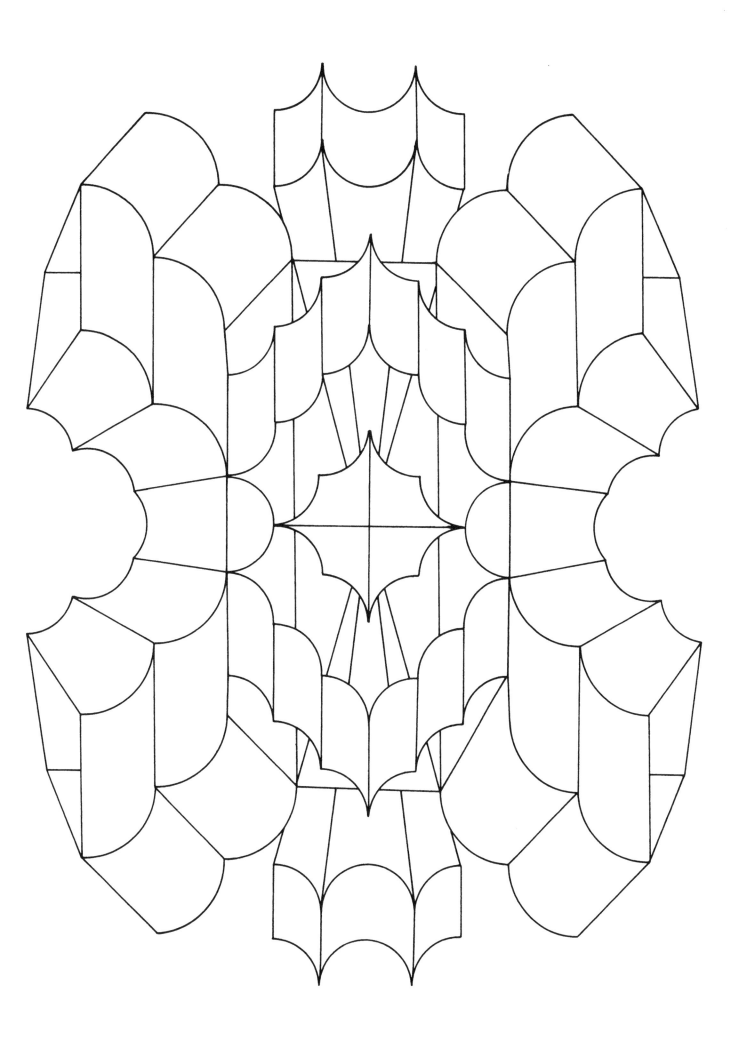

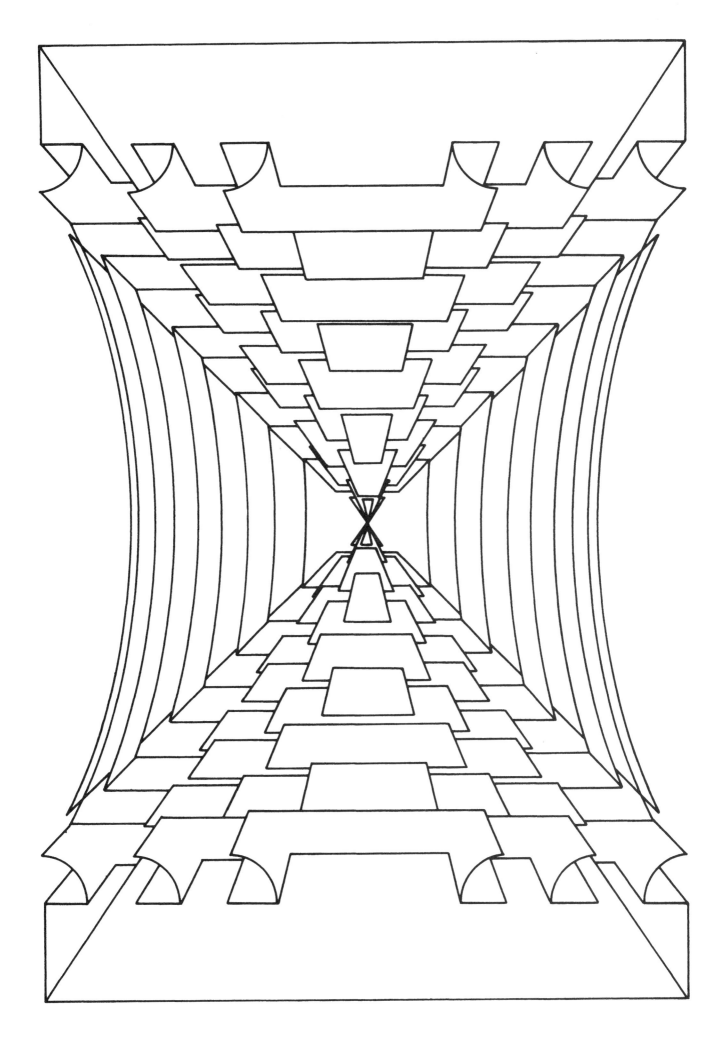

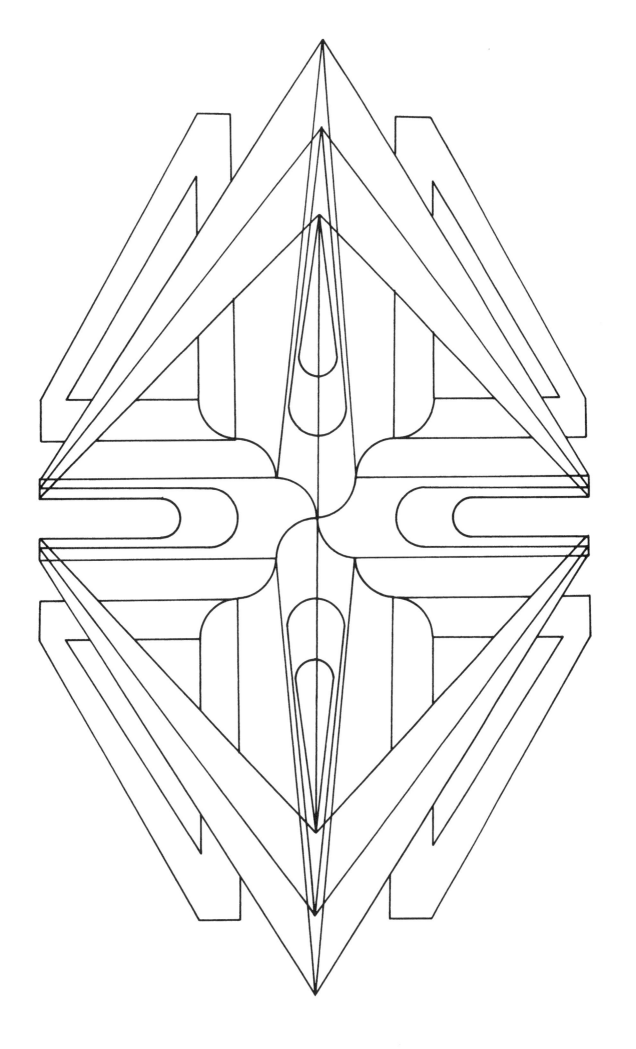

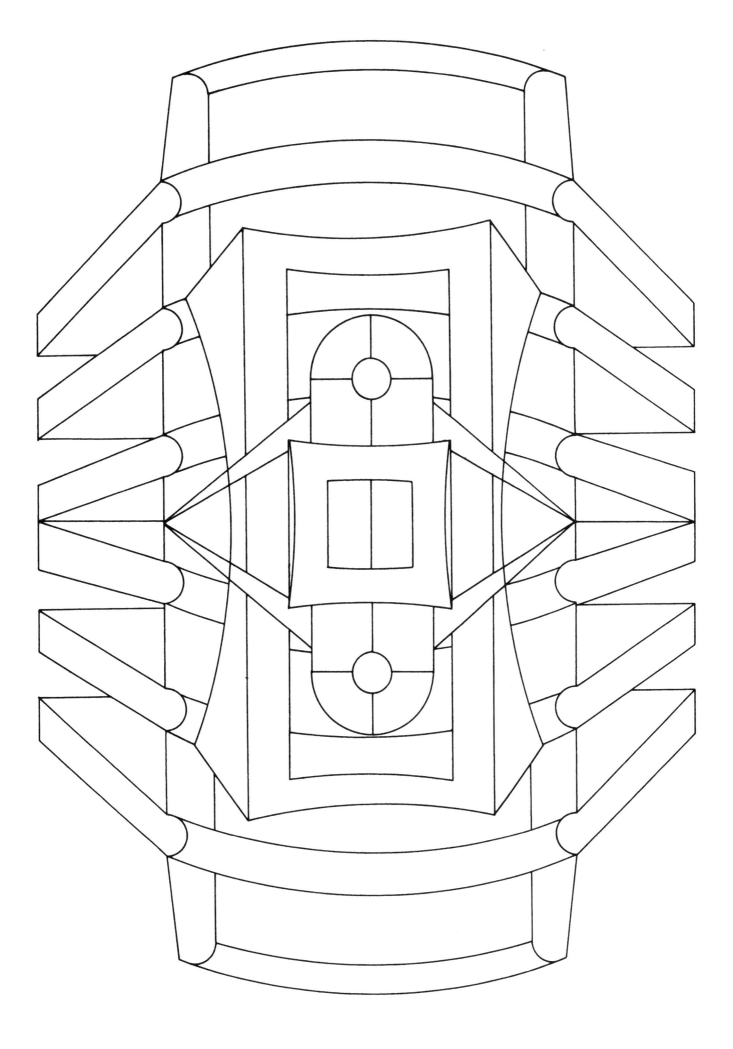

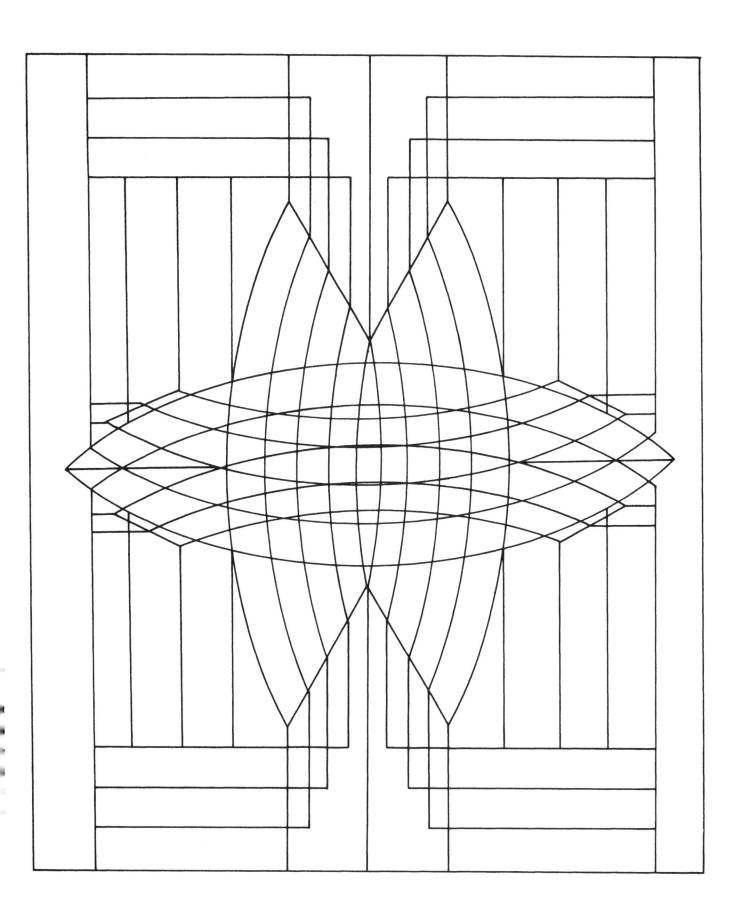

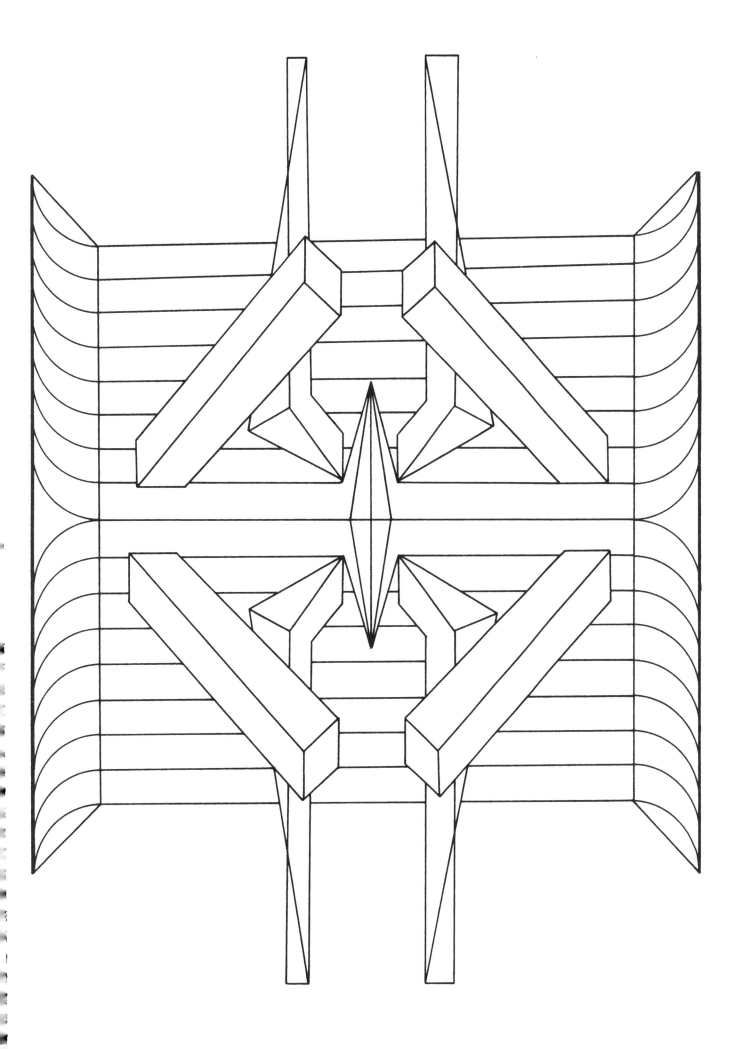

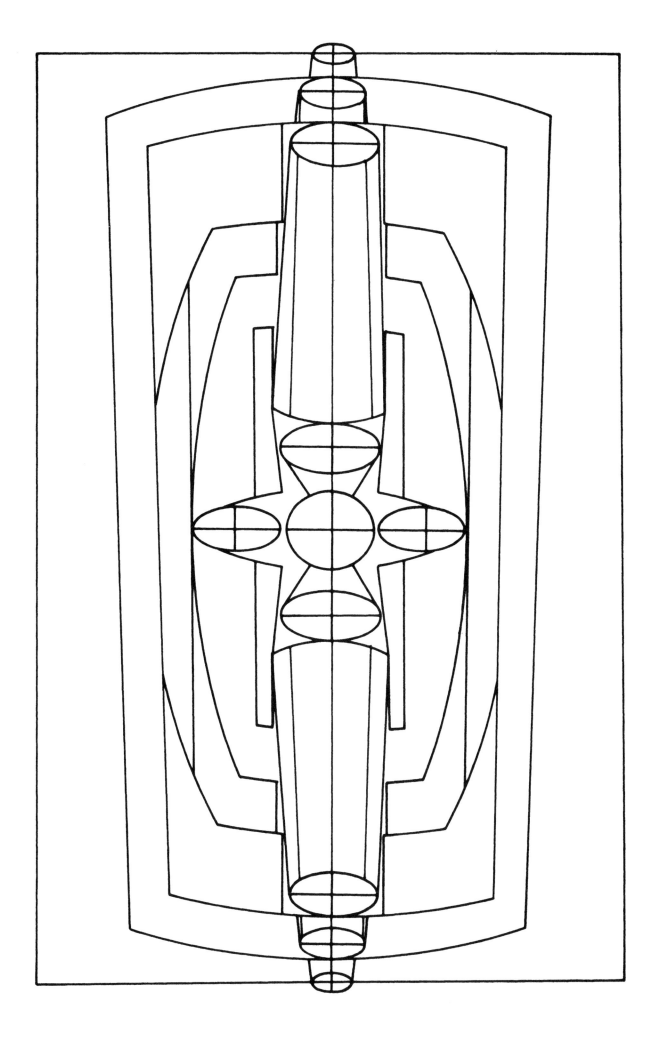

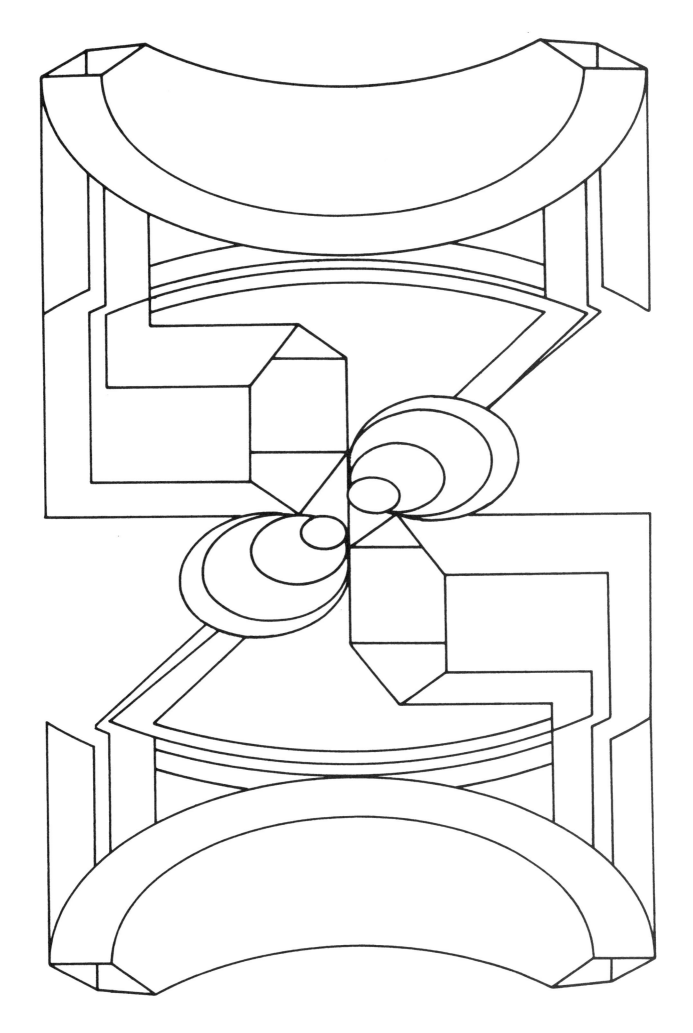

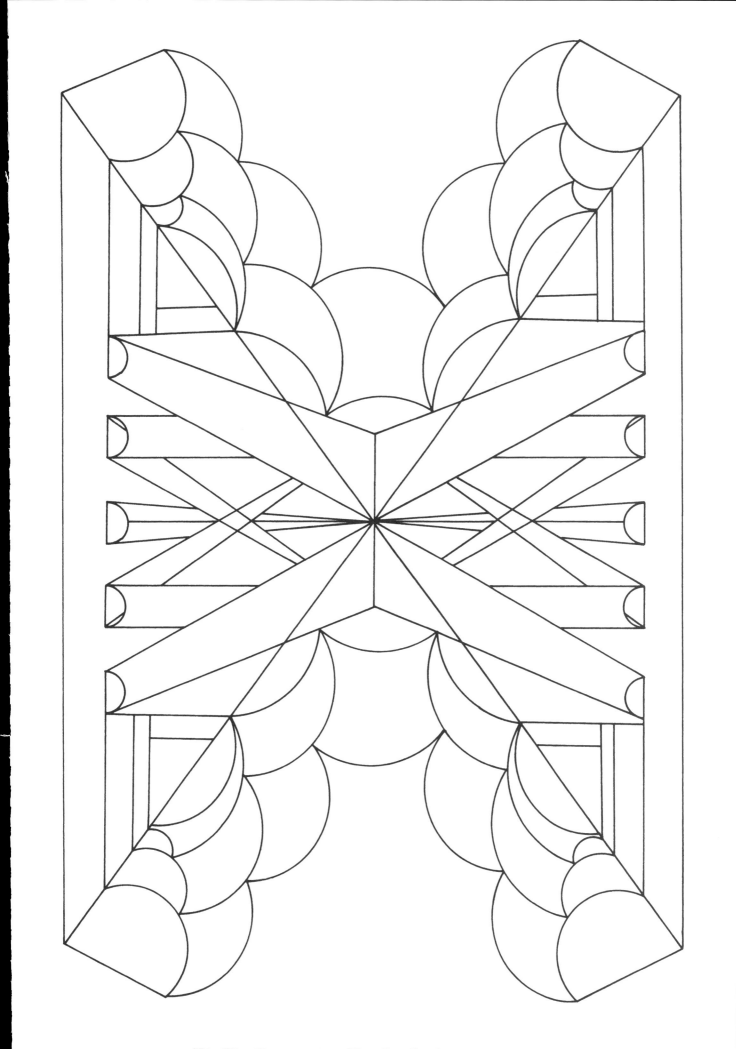

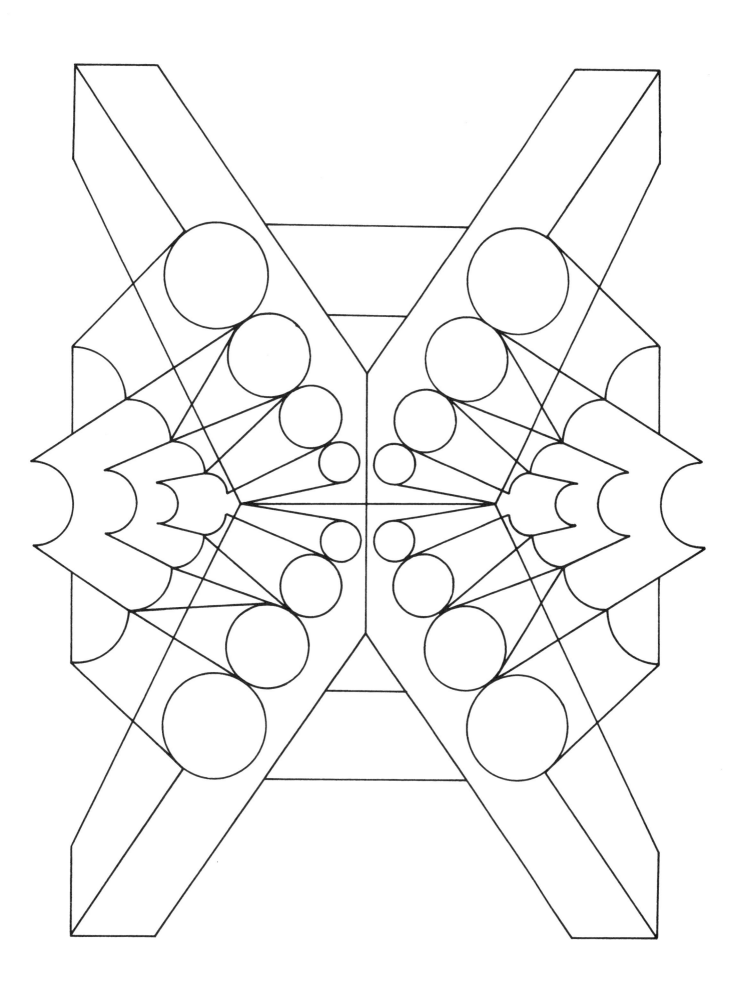

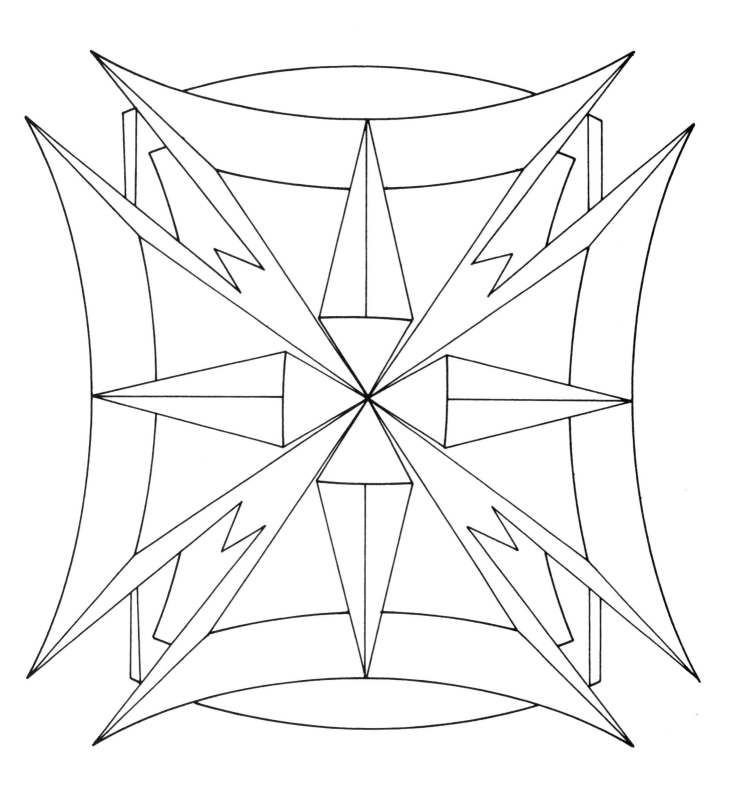

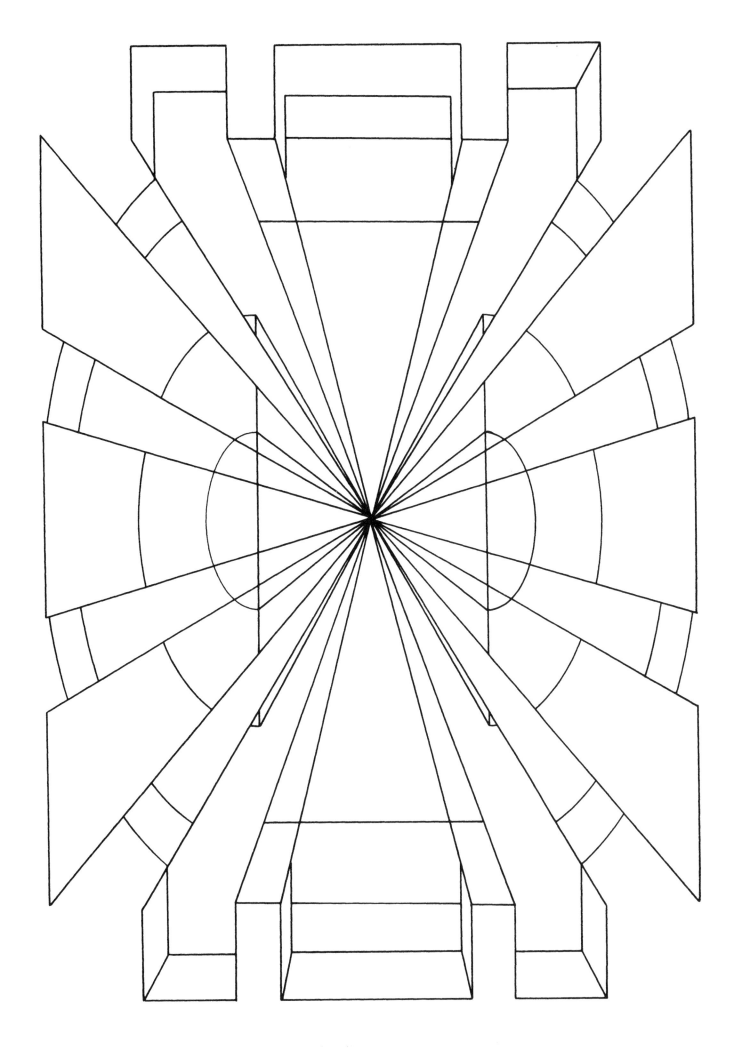